Additional Praise for *Why Bother With ...*

"Over the past several years, as stocks have surged and bond yields have dwindled, investors increasingly ask "Why bother with bonds?" Rick Van Ness takes this question and runs with it in his book sporting this provocative title. Sooner or later, this question will answer itself, and it will behoove all investors to get to know Rick before it does. Read it, enjoy it, and profit from it—before it's too late."

William J. Bernstein
Author, *The Investor's Manifesto,* and
The Four Pillars of Investing

"Every successful portfolio includes bonds. Having the right bond strategy will serve to carry investors through the inevitable stock market meltdowns. Having the wrong bond strategy, however, will prove financially fatal. In his simply stated and entertaining book, Rick Van Ness eloquently instructs the reader on how to do bonds right – in fact, better than any single book I've read. *Why Bother with Bonds* dispels many bond myths, giving readers an insight that could be the difference between achieving financial independence or not."

Allan S. Roth, CFP®, CPA, MBA
Author: *How a Second Grader Beat Wall Street*

"*Why Bother with Bonds?*" is one of the most asked questions on the Bogleheads Forum. In his great little book of the same name, Rick Van Ness answers this important question in words and graphs. Rick provides the information needed to select the best type and amount of bonds necessary to provide safety and income for one's portfolio.

Taylor Larimore
Co-author, *The Bogleheads' Guide to Investing,* and
The Bogleheads' Guide to Retirement Planning

"This book should be part of America's high school curriculum."

Andrew Hallam
Author, *Millionaire Teacher*

"If you are a DIY investor . . . you should read this book. It will steer you clear of areas you need to avoid and into where you should be. A quick read filled with valuable info!"

Robert Wasilewski
President, RW Investment Strategies

WHY BOTHER WITH BONDS

Also by Rick Van Ness

Common Sense Investing
Ten Simple Rules to Finance Your Dreams

WHY BOTHER WITH BONDS

A Guide To Build An All-Weather Portfolio
Including CDs, Bonds, and Bond Funds
—Even During Low Interest Rates

(First Edition)

Rick Van Ness

Foreword by Larry Swedroe

Published by GrowthConnection, LLC
Mukilteo, Washington, USA

Author Online

Find explanatory videos, smart tips,
and links to useful resources at
www.FinancingLife.org
rick@financinglife.org

Use of Proceeds

100% of the revenue from sales of this book will be applied towards promoting financial literacy through bite-sized videos, short books, and other educational projects.

Comments and feedback welcomed and appreciated!

The author welcomes and appreciates all thoughts and suggestions. Reach him at: rick@financinglife.org.

ISBN: 978-0985800406 (Paperback)

Library of Congress Control Number: 2013939289

Printed in the United States of America.
Version 1.02

Dedication

To John C. Bogle, champion of ordinary investors, who points out the common sense amid all the noise and confusion. You helped me see the difference between investing and speculating, and the genius in common sense.

~ ~ ~

To all Bogleheads. I learn from each of you. And more than anything, you've been excellent role models—generously sharing your wisdom, often anonymously.

~ ~ ~

To each of you readers who have selected this book because your dreams will need money. May all your dreams come true!

Table of Contents

Classic Investor Stew

Key Ingredients:
- Beef (or, U.S. stocks)
- Potatoes (or, U.S. Treasury bonds)
- Carrots (or, International stocks)
- Water (or, your emergency fund)(*liquid asset—ha ha*)

Foreword

Despite its obvious importance to every individual, our education system almost totally ignores the field of finance and investments. Consequently most Americans, having taken a course in English literature in high school, have more knowledge about William Shakespeare than they do about investing.

The result is that individuals are making investments without the basic knowledge required to understand the implications of their decisions. As humorist Josh Billings noted: "It ain't what a man don't know as makes him a fool, but what he does know as ain't so."

When most investors begin their investment journey they focus on equity investing; bond investing is often an afterthought. This is unfortunate because for most individuals bond investing plays an essential role in their overall investment strategy. Think of it this way, if your portfolio was a stew, fixed-income securities would be a main ingredient, like potatoes or carrots, not just a seasoning (e.g., salt, pepper) you add but might be able to leave out without adversely affecting the quality of the stew.

It is also unfortunate that many investors erroneously base their ideas and assumptions about investing in bonds on their "knowledge" of equities. As Rick explains, the two are completely different asset classes with different characteristics; even if the investor's thought process is correct on the equity side it may not be correct in the case of fixed income.

While education can be expensive, ignorance is generally far more costly, especially in the investment world — a world filled with hungry wolves waiting to devour the innocent sheep. Benjamin Franklin said, "An investment in knowledge pays the best interest." Your investment in knowledge is the price of Rick's book and the time you invest in reading it. The interest you receive will be the knowledge you need to be an informed bond investor. Informed investors generally make far better investment decisions. And being an informed investor will help prevent you from being exploited by investment firms that take advantage of the lack of knowledge the general public has about investing in bonds. The result is that it is more likely that you will be the one with the yacht, and not your broker.

LARRY E. SWEDROE

Larry Swedroe is author of *The Only Guide to a Winning Investment Strategy You'll Ever Need,* 13 other investment books, and the Director of Research for Buckingham Asset Management and the BAM Alliance.

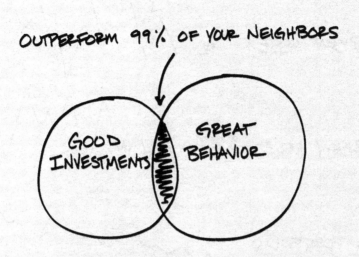

OUTPERFORM 99% OF YOUR NEIGHBORS

GOOD INVESTMENTS

GREAT BEHAVIOR

Sketch by Carl Richards at BehaviorGap.com

Many of you have picked up this book wondering, Why bonds? The answer is about risks—about owning the appropriate amount of low-risk assets whose payoff time scale *matches your needs*. Bonds are a key ingredient in all good investment portfolios, and the part that assures great investor behavior.

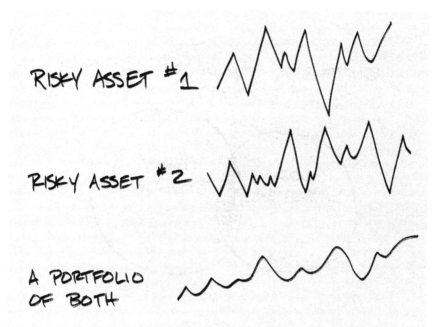

RISKY ASSET #1

RISKY ASSET #2

A PORTFOLIO OF BOTH

Sketch by Carl Richards at BehaviorGap.com

Introduction

Who Should Read This Book?

Read this book if you want to learn time-proven wisdom about both short- and long-term investing. Maybe you have heard that you should invest in "broadly diversified index funds at the lowest possible cost." But, what does *that* mean? Don't worry. I'm going to show you, and it is not hard. But there is more! Let me show you some of the valuable reasons why it is important to include *bonds* in your investing.

Protect Your Investments From Yourself

Consider Fred and Chuck. They've both been faithfully investing 15% of every paycheck since the year 2000. Fred was aggressive. He chose to invest 100% in stocks, and he wisely chose a broadly diversified low-cost index fund. The stock market began to plummet early in the summer of 2008, and he began worrying. On September 25, presidential candidate John McCain suspended his campaign to fly to Washington, D.C. to address the ominous financial crisis. Enough! Fred traded his 100% stock investment for a more balanced portfolio (60% stocks/40% bonds). It was worth $84,000 that day, down from a peak of $150,000 early that year. It was an emotion-based decision that cost him dearly.

Chuck likes things simple. He hates to stress about financial decisions, so he invested exactly the same amounts on the same days into that same 60/40 balanced fund. When Fred's investment was down 44% in late 2008, Chuck's was down only 31%. He hung on, and despite the ever-present drumbeat of bad news in the news, he never had a bad night's sleep. His investments were worth $13,000 more than Fred on that sorry day, but have grown to be worth $25,500 more than Fred today (June 2014)—and the difference is growing exponentially. This is what you can do! I'll teach you how to reduce the risk of letting your emotions ruin your investing.

Reduce Financial Risk For Known Spending Needs

Sam has a story of being lured into carrying too much investment risk. Growth in the stock market made him think he could retire comfortably. He looked forward to retiring in 2010 and was going to invest more conservatively then—since he would no longer have an income. Meanwhile, he just wanted to grow that nest egg a little bigger while he could. But the 2008 financial crisis was accompanied with massive layoffs. He got laid off—down-sized, involuntarily retired—but his nest egg that was nearly adequate a year before was now substantially short of meeting his needs. He tried to get a job for the next two years and eventually just lowered his standard of living to match what he could now afford. It's not what he had wanted.

It's Your Most Important Investment Decision

Ask yourself this: "What is your most important investment decision?"

- Which stock to buy?
- What to buy?
- When to sell?
- Choosing your stock broker?
- How much of your income to save?
- How to allocate your investing between stocks and bonds?

Two of these answers rise to the top. But I assert that only one wins.

Key point: Your *allocation between stocks and bonds* is your most important investment <u>decision</u>.

Yep, it's *that* important. But don't worry, I'm going to make it easy for you. This book is all about finding and managing that allocation.

Arguably, deciding to live below your means is equally important since you have to constantly make the lifestyle choice. I like to say:

Key: *Saving part of every paycheck* is your most important <u>habit</u>.

This book explains why CDs, bonds, and bond funds have a role in every investor's portfolio—even in an environment of exceptionally low interest rates. It illuminates how to rely on stocks and the miracle of compound interest to achieve those big long-term goals, but it is bonds that *control risk* in short- and medium-term money and ensure that you will have the amount of money you need when you need it.

It's a practical guide. In addition to removing the mysteries, I identify common misconceptions and attempt to explain simple truths in plain English. My premise is that most people can, and should, understand these.

Start with a Sound Financial Lifestyle

Financial success starts with living below your means (spending less than you earn), and developing a sound financial lifestyle. My first book, Common Sense Investing, describes ten guiding principles for investing wisely to finance your dreams. These are also generally regarded as the Bogleheads® Investment Philosophy at the popular investment website which I both support and highly recommend.

The site is arguably the internet's best discussion board and wiki for personal investing advice. Wisdom is shared and explained by generous and knowledgeable experts. Here, tens of thousands of participants endearingly call themselves Bogleheads to honor John C. Bogle, lifelong champion for ordinary investors and inventor of the world's first index fund.

Mr. Bogle is also legendary for founding Vanguard, a discount investment house organized as a *cooperative* owned by all mutual fund investors (like you) which keeps costs low.

My short books and free online videos are my small contribution to spreading their wisdom and helping people finance their dreams. This proven investment philosophy can be summarized as ten simple rules:

> Rule #1. Develop a workable plan
> Rule #2. Invest early and often
> Rule #3. Never bear too much or too little risk
> Rule #4. Diversify
> Rule #5. Never try to time the market
> Rule #6. Use index funds when possible
> Rule #7. Keep costs low

Rule #8. Minimize taxes
Rule #9. Keep it simple
Rule #10. Stay the course

Common Sense Investing, explains these rules and encourages you to *create a personal plan* and *put it in writing.* Start where you are, and start now. I still cannot overemphasize the importance of this. People that don't develop a plan and commit to it are the ones most likely to make costly investment mistakes. It can be as simple as hand written on a single side of paper.

Key point: Start with a first draft. You can always change it later! Take small steps. *Better beats perfect.*

Sidebar: Meet The Bogleheads

Learn from, or join, the lively but respectful investing discussion forum here:

www.Bogleheads.org

Generous contributions from many wise contributors make this wikipedia about investing one of the gems on the internet:

www.Bogleheads.org/wiki

For young investors, *savings rate* is more important than all the other investing advice we talk about. Savings rate is the percentage of your gross income that you set aside for future years. As important as it is to start investing early, it is even more important to start with a *sound financial lifestyle.* It means acquiring health insurance, car insurance, and possibly life insurance if you have dependents. Your first savings should be an emergency fund and possibly earmarked savings for a car, wedding, house. Investing is all about financing your dreams. It's not hard, but it does require a smart understanding about assuming *investment risk* to overcome inflation and reap the investment returns.

Sidebar: What is Risk?

Boiled down to the essence, our concern is about <u>money not being</u> <u>there when we need it</u>. It is the overarching theme of this book. At times, we substitute "price volatility" as an indication of risk. Often, it's very useful. But it's not perfect. It's rarely a problem when the value of your investment abruptly jumps, but it can be devastating when the value suddenly tanks.

In Rule #3 we describe how your allocation between stocks and bonds is your *most important investment decision.* No other factor controls your investment risk and return as much as this decision. We usually consider all your investments as a whole and then speak of it as a ratio—for instance, 60/40 to refer to 60% stocks and 40% bonds.

Stocks and bonds are the two key ingredients for success. Stocks, yes! But bonds? When I started to write this book in 2012, almost all Treasury bonds had a negative yield after expected inflation. Negative! We'll start with this most pressing question: Why bother with bonds?

Sidebar: Free Videos Accompany This Book

Find and share my free videos at

www.FinancingLife.org

and

www.YouTube.com/FinancingLife101

INVESTING DONE RIGHT

WATCHING GRASS GROW

BOTH ARE BORING!

Sketch by Carl Richards at BehaviorGap.com

Why Bother With Bonds?

KEY CONCEPTS:

- **Stocks are much riskier.**

- **Bonds make risk more palatable.**

- **High-quality bonds can be a safe bet.**

- **Bonds are an attractive diversifier.**

Smart investing is not just about which investment will give you the highest returns—you can always find a higher risk investment that promises higher expected returns—it's about selecting levels of risk/reward that match your various needs.

We have the competing objectives of achieving inflation-adjusted long-term growth while gradually decreasing risk as our investment timeframe decreases.

Our goal is to always safeguard the money we expect to need in the short-term while achieving growth, in excess of inflation, to create the future we desire. CDs, bonds, and bond funds—when chosen correctly—are uniquely well-suited to help us accomplish both. Four compelling arguments keep them vital for your investment portfolio: stocks are very risky, bonds make that risk more palatable, bonds are a safe bet, and bonds are an attractive diversifier.

Stocks are risky in the short run, and the long run too!

What if the stock market tanks—right before you need the money?

The first reason why owning some bonds is always important is because stocks are very risky. If we pay any attention to the news, then we know they are volatile. Remember Sam from the Introduction? His story is all too common. It's easy to accept too much risk when the market is rising. Here's a good rule of thumb:

Key point: *Stocks could lose 50% or more of their value in any year.*

That year could be this year, or the first year after you retire—so they are risky in the short term and the long term as well.

Investors expect to be compensated with higher returns for carrying that risk. Over the past two centuries, stocks have returned 7% per year above inflation—or a real return twice that of bonds.[1,2] The return above inflation is called the "real return" and that's what matters.

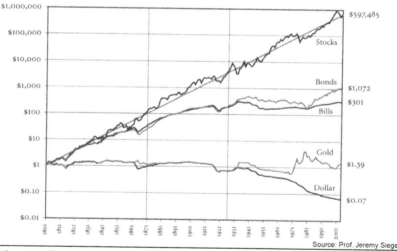

Total Real Return on $10,000 Initial Investment (1802-2003)

Stocks outperform bonds in the long run—because they are riskier.

Charts like the one above are called Hypothetical Return on $10,000 invested because they show total return—both growth in price plus dividends reinvested—and allow you to compare different kinds of investments. This chart is unusual in that it covers such a long history and thus requires a logarithmic scale, but it makes a strong point that, historically, stock returns have been higher than bonds.

But doesn't this just beg our very question: Why bother with bonds? One important time is when you can be hurt by short-term volatility. The ratio of stocks to bonds is the most important lever you have to control your overall investment risk.

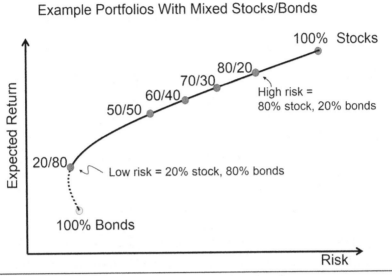

Example Portfolios With Mixed Stocks/Bonds

In a diversified portfolio, the ratio of stocks/bonds controls risk.

This figure shows both how investors expect greater returns for increased investment risk and also how they can control the ratio of stocks to bonds to control their risk exposure. Later in this book we will learn why most investors want to own 20% to 80% bonds.

Bonds are risky too. Later we'll see that bond values move opposite interest rates and sometimes don't keep up with inflation. But keep this in perspective! They are an order of magnitude less volatile than stocks and we'll learn how these risks can be managed.

Here's a question for you to consider. Which of these is true?

    (1) The longer you own stocks, the safer they become.
    (2) The longer you own bonds, the safer they become.

Did you choose "stocks get safer"?

If we use volatility to measure safety, then this one is false. Stocks remain volatile every day of every year, including the day before you sell them 40 years from now. But this is an easy mistake to make because we often hear that "stocks held for decades rarely lose money." That's true too, but not losing the amount you originally invested becomes less important than not losing the value it grows to become—and that you come to rely on.

Did you choose "bonds get safer"?

This is correct. These two choices get at a major difference. While buying stocks is buying ownership in companies—something you can keep forever—buying a bond is really just loaning your money for a specific period of time. The longer you own the bond, the closer you get to the maturity date, at which time you will (hopefully) get back the full value that you invested. The highest quality bonds are very safe with no surprises.

Later on we'll look at CDs, bond funds, and other ways to own bonds that have some differences to be aware of. But next, we'll look at how bonds can provide welcome ballast to stabilize your portfolio in a bad year.

Bonds Make Risk More Palatable

Buy high and sell low? Bonds can help prevent that.

We already saw that stocks are both attractive, and risky. A second reason to own some bonds is to make that stock market risk more palatable. An allocation to bonds moderates the short-term volatility of stocks.

I mentioned Fred, in the Introduction, and how he bailed out at the height of the 2008 financial crisis. It is sometimes hard for others—when you're not in their shoes—to imagine doing this. So I've included this next chart showing the total return of the same stock fund. It is easier to imagine why Fred felt so terrible that he could not sleep. The value at its peak was fixed in his head. The future looked like it might get worse—in fact, it did. Fred got out four months before the bottom.[3]

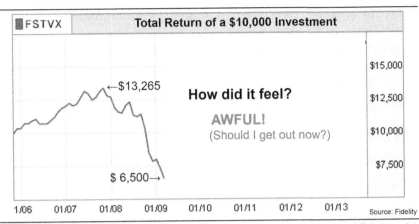

Here's how a $10,000 investment in stocks felt in Feb 2009: awful! Stocks fell 51% in 16 months.

Too many panicked after the market tumbled and sold at a loss. Remember: newspapers, magazines, and television shows all amplify the hysteria that cause some to sell their stocks. That emotion-based bad decision might have been prevented if that investor owned a bigger allotment of high-quality bonds.

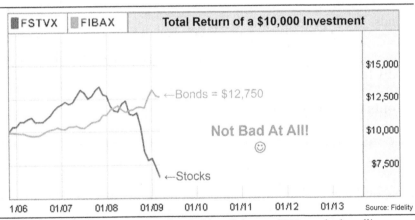

Here's how a $10,000 investment in bonds felt in February 2009: not bad at all! U.S. Treasury Bonds provide stability during downturns.

Here's what happened to an equal investment in Treasury bonds over this same period. It did great, but probably most important is if it kept that investor from panic selling during a bad year. Bonds give the risk-averse long-term investor the courage and confidence to "stay the course" when the market periodically tumbles.

It is healthy to view bonds as the foundation of your portfolio—a moderating influence on a stock portfolio. Dr. William Bernstein once surprised me by calling bonds "the underwear in your portfolio."[4] But, I like that analogy.

We'd never say, "Bonds are the jewelry in your portfolio." No one is going to brag about their bonds at a party, although they might brag about some stock they got lucky with or show off their jewelry.

The full quote by Dr. William Bernstein is "Bonds are the underwear in your portfolio—unexciting and not much thought about, but select the wrong pair and you'll be surprised at just how uncomfortable you are." Perfect! Because this section is all about planning to take as much risk as you comfortably can, after considering your goals and circumstances, and then sticking with your plan no matter what happens in the stock market. Dr. Bernstein made this comment when addressing whether to buy bonds that will mature in the short term or the long term. But I also like it because it applies to choosing between high-quality bonds or high-yield bonds. We'll get to all that later.

But first, I have asserted that bonds can be a very safe bet. Is that really true?

Bonds Can Be A Safe Bet

The value of bonds goes down when interest rates go up, so how's that a safe bet?

The third reason why owning some bonds is always important is that bonds can be a safe bet—and by that I mean "no surprises." With any bond or CD, you loan your money for a specific period of time in exchange for periodic interest payments on specific dates of fixed amounts. And then at the end of the term you get your full investment back. In some cases, this is all guaranteed by the government—that's pretty safe.

What can go wrong? Well, you can get into trouble by chasing after high-yield bonds from companies with low credit ratings. These are called "junk bonds" and they tend to get in trouble at the same times the stock market does—the very time you most want some stability. You can also have a problem if you lock your money up for a long term and then need it before the bonds mature.

Key point: The strategy I like, is to *choose a fund of high-quality bonds that will add stability to your investment portfolio* when the stock market plummets.

The thinking behind this strategy is that you'll get better overall return by taking your investment risk on the stock side of your portfolio.[5]

How is your understanding of risk? Which of these is true?

> (1) If you hold a bond (or a CD) to maturity, you still have interest rate risk.
> (2) U.S. Treasury Bonds, or FDIC-insured CDs, are risk-free investments.

Did you choose "risk-free investments"? This one is false. These do have impeccable credit risk, meaning they will pay you exactly as agreed (all the interest payments and then you'll get 100% of your invested principal), but they still have interest rate risk. Interest rate risk means the value of your bond changes when interest rates change. All bonds, including all CDs, have interest rate risk, which is why the first fact is true.

Did you choose "still have interest rate risk"? Yes! This is true. But it confounds a lot of people how you can have any risk from changing interest rates if you get all your interest payments and then 100% of your invested principal on the dates promised.

Let's look at a simple example to help you see this. Suppose you purchase two bonds. The first bond you purchase yields 5%. The next day, bad luck, interest rates rise 1% and you buy a second bond. At 6%, it's worth $10 more at maturity. That makes Bond 1 instantly worth $9.43 less than what you paid and that grows to the $10 difference at maturity.[6]

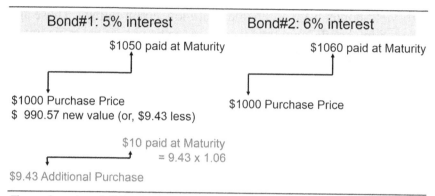

Bond#1: 5% interest	Bond#2: 6% interest

$1050 paid at Maturity $1060 paid at Maturity

$1000 Purchase Price $1000 Purchase Price
$ 990.57 new value (or, $9.43 less)

$10 paid at Maturity
= 9.43 x 1.06

$9.43 Additional Purchase

The market value of all bonds change with interest rates by an amount governed by simple arithmetic.

Another way to look at it is: you would need to invest $9.43 at the new interest rate to be equal to the $10 additional that the second bond pays.

Yes, <u>all bonds have interest rate risk</u>. So how can that be a safe bet? Because there were no surprises. You got exactly what you expected, and what was promised, when you purchased each of these!

Later, we will show how to choose bonds that will protect yourself from both interest rate changes, and from inflation. But next we're going to see the important bonus you get because bonds often "ying" when stocks "yang".

Bonds Are An Attractive Investment Diversifier

Treasury bond returns are uncorrelated with stock returns. What does that mean? And, why is it important?

Our fourth reason why owning bonds is important is that bonds can be an attractive diversifier in your portfolio. Not only do bonds dilute the amount of the portfolio at risk in the stock market, but the portfolio is strengthened. High-quality bonds are poorly correlated with the stock market so the total portfolio earns a better return for any given level of risk.

Key point: Another useful rule of thumb is that <u>everyone should</u>

own between 20% and 80% bonds.

This chart shows that a typical portfolio with 60% stocks and 40% bonds doesn't fall 30% when the stock market falls 50%—rather something significantly less.[7]

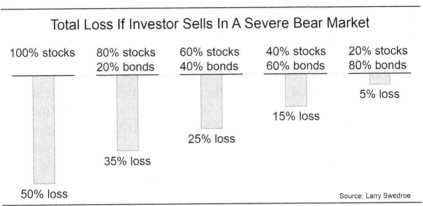

Total Loss If Investor Sells In A Severe Bear Market

100% stocks	80% stocks 20% bonds	60% stocks 40% bonds	40% stocks 60% bonds	20% stocks 80% bonds

5% loss

15% loss

25% loss

35% loss

50% loss

Source: Larry Swedroe

Your overall ratio of stocks to bonds is the primary lever that controls volatility.

This is a magical benefit for you, but first let's understand the concept. Correlation is a measure of whether stocks and bond prices move together, or independently from each other.

Ideally, we would find two investments that had attractive average returns, but where one had a good year exactly when the other had a bad one. On a scale of -1 to +1, these would be very negative, but unfortunately these only exist in our dreams.

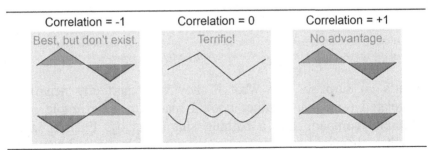

Correlation = -1	Correlation = 0	Correlation = +1
Best, but don't exist.	Terrific!	No advantage.

High-quality bonds provide extra value to investors because they are poorly correlated (near zero) with stocks.

Uncorrelated, or poorly correlated, means they are independent from each other. This is terrific. Things that move in the same direction at the same time are perfectly positively correlated. An example below, with actual market data, illustrates how correlations observed over short time periods is worthless. Long periods, over 20 years, are required to identify trends that have any predictive value.

Now before we get to the magic I've promised, we need to introduce one more thing: we need a way to describe the volatility of these returns.

The average annual return is the *expected value*. It's useful and valuable, but it doesn't indicate volatility. So we use this measure called *standard deviation* to describe the distribution of returns. It simply means that the total return will be within one standard deviation in either direction, roughly 7 out of every 10 years—or in this case within the range from -10% to +30%. Further, it means that the total return will be within two standard deviations for 95 out of every 100 years. Now let's put it all together.

To illustrate two perfectly correlated funds let's combine the S&P500 fund from one company with the S&P500 fund from another. Presumably they are perfectly correlated and the combination is a weighted average.

	Expected Return					
	Average ± Std. Dev.					
Vanguard S&P 500 Index Fund:	+10 %	±20%		Correlation		
Fidelity S&P 500 Index Fund:	+10 %	±20%	-1	0	+1
Combination:	+10 %	±20%			

The result of combining perfectly correlated assets is simply the weighted average of the assets. Anything less than perfect +1 correlation produces a superior portfolio.

That's no surprise. But what if they were perfectly negatively correlated (-1)? For another book I made up an example of an umbrella company and a bathing suit company. Each time the weather changed, sales at one company got better and the other company got worse. I used these to illustrate how two risky assets could be combined in a proportion that eliminated volatility altogether. Sadly, negative correlation is near impossible to find.

16

Here's the part that is important: *adding any asset with anything less than +1 correlation always provides better risk-return opportunities than the individual assets on their own.*

	Total Annual Return		
	Average	±	Std. Dev.
Stock Market:	+10 %		±20%
Fund B:	+10 %		±20%
Equal Combination:	+10 %		±14%

Correlation
-1   0   +1

Portfolio volatility (risk) falls as correlation becomes less positive.

For example, here we combine an equal amount of two funds with the same expected return and the same volatility that are completely uncorrelated, meaning the movements are completely independent and unaffected by each other. The standard deviation becomes less than the weighted average. The combination is better than the individual funds on their own. Wow, where do you find an uncorrelated fund like that? The short answer is: bonds. The longer answer includes a warning that the correlation of two assets depends on the time period they are compared.

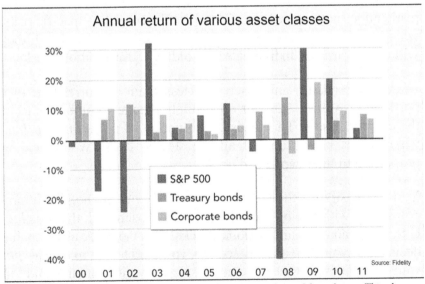

Annual return of various asset classes

Source: Fidelity

Only long-term correlations of broad asset classes provide useful guidance. This shows how short-term variations can be misleading.

This chart[8] reveals that only long-term correlations of broad asset

17

classes have any predictive power for our investments in the future. Consider these correlations over three time periods:

- In the three years 2000 – 2002, stock returns went down but bond returns went up.
- In the four years 2003 – 2006, stocks went up and bonds went up too.
- And in the years 2008-2009, corporate bonds moved in the same direction as stocks, but Treasury bonds moved opposite.

Key point: The only useful correlation information comes from comparing asset classes over long periods of time.

Key point: U.S. Treasury bond returns have almost no correlation with stock returns—adding valuable stability to an investment portfolio. Being uncorrelated (near zero) means their values move independently from each other—but that doesn't preclude that sometimes they move in the same direction.

It turns out that to own individual stocks is to carry risk that the market does not compensate.[9] These are the company-specific risks, which can be diversified away. And since other investors will, they will not reward any individuals for holding these additional risks.

In theory[10], adding any asset with less than +1 correlation to a portfolio provides a superior opportunity than any combinations of the existing assets. This leads to the notion of a *best mutual fund* which is an index fund of all the stocks of the world held in proportion to their capitalization.

You can easily do this and be diversified both economically and politically, with one or two mutual funds chosen such that it is *half* U.S. stocks and *half* international stocks. This would be a reasonable decision. If you have a US-based job, you might want to *overweight* your international stocks to compensate for your "human capital in a U.S. firm." But, reasons to *underweight* international stocks might be for expense reasons, or that they are slightly less tax efficient. Bottom line: choose a proportion of international stocks to be 30-

50% of your total stocks, and then *stick to it*.

The portfolio examples in the last chapter of this book illustrate some specific funds to achieve worldwide diversification of the stock side of your portfolio. Now, what about the bond side?

Should you diversify your bonds in the same way? I discuss that later, but here's a hint: no. Treasuries have the highest credit quality and do not require diversification. Diversifying bonds is quite different than diversifying stocks.

The bond side of your portfolio could be single bond, say a 5-year FDIC-insured CD. Or, it could be several. Also coming up, we'll talk about diversifying the term of your bonds. Here again the reasons are completely different than with stocks.

To finish our discussion on correlation, would you like to try a harder question? Which of these is true?

(1) High-yield bonds are less correlated with the stock market than U.S. Treasury bonds.
(2) Choosing stocks and bonds that are uncorrelated give investors a "free lunch".

Did you choose "high-yield bonds are less correlated than Treasuries"? It isn't true. But that's OK, because I only made a brief comment on this. Junk bonds, or bonds issued by companies with poor credit ratings, are euphemistically called "high yield" bonds and are sold to investors chasing after the highest yield for their bond holdings. These are more positively correlated with the stock market, and often perform poorly at the very time you need their stability.

Did you choose "the free lunch"? This is true. The overall net result is to get more return for the same amount of volatility, or risk. That's the free lunch. While moving in opposite directions at the same time would be ideal; being uncorrelated, or even poorly correlated, is very good. This is why high-quality bonds are an attractive diversifier.

19

Next, learn more about bonds, bond funds, and tips about how to use them.

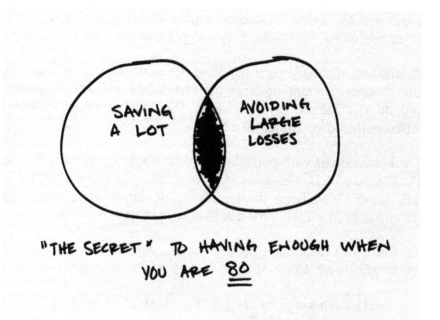

Life Is Complicated;
Bonds Are Not.

Should you choose a money market fund or a bond fund? Or perhaps dividend-paying stocks?

At first glance, some investing options look similar. Consider this: which types of investment will give you both a stable income stream and keep the principal at a stable value? In other words, if you have $40,000, is there a way to invest it such that every month they'd pay you a fixed amount, say $100, but at any time you desire you could stop and get your $40,000 back?

Suppose we want both: a <u>stable income stream</u> and maintain a <u>stable principal value</u>. Would you look for:

- a money market fund?
- a bond?
- a dividend-paying stock?
- or none of these?

Make your best guess. Choose one, and then I'll tell you the answer.

Did you choose "a dividend-paying stock"?

Stocks pay dividends. Buying a stock is buying ownership in a company. You can own it forever. You might wonder about whether these dividends are like bond dividends—after all, they are both called dividends, and both are payments on specific dates. But stock dividends are not contractual obligations with stockholders—they can be changed at any time, even eliminated. And the value of the stock moves with the stock market. No guarantees, but probably not the best answer to our thought problem.

Dividend-paying Stock

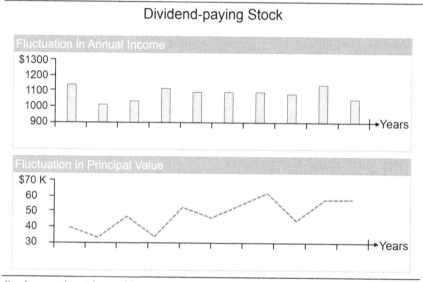

Stocks provide neither stable income nor stable principal value.

Did you choose "a money market fund"?

A money market fund does guarantee to protect your investment. It's a perfect place to stash your cash for a short term. You can always get back your investment, plus they pay you some interest for that money every month. But, the interest rate varies so it cannot be relied upon to provide a stable income stream.

Money Market Fund

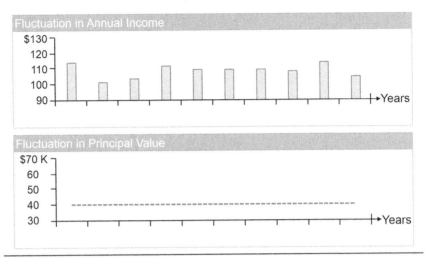

A money market fund preserves capital, but interest rate fluctuates.

Did you choose "a bond"?

Bonds do that. They are a simple loan for a fixed length of time, and in return you get a fixed dividend every period and your money returned at the end of the term. So, bonds can assure you a stable income stream, but the market value of the bond can fluctuate over the term. In fact, it varies every time interest rates change. The price wanders in a totally unpredictable direction (since you can't predict interest rate changes) but gradually drifts towards that one date when you're guaranteed to get your investment back, the end of the term when the bond matures.

Long-term Government Bond

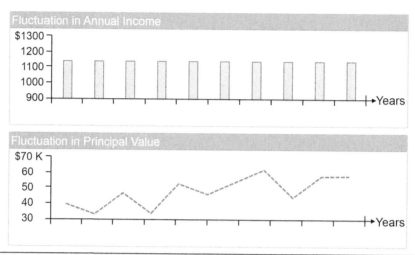

Bonds provide a stable income stream, but the principal value varies with interest rates.

Did you choose "none of these"?

Correct. It's "none of these." So, to summarize: You can have stable income stream or stable principal value, but you cannot have them both.[11] This is a primary distinction between a bond and a money market fund.

Investors can either buy an ownership stake in a company, or lend their money using vehicles such as a money market, CDs, or bonds. Now let's take a closer look.

What is a Money Market Fund?

KEY CONCEPTS:

- Money markets are set up so that the value of one share is constant ($1.00) but the interest rate varies.

- Bonds, and bond funds, provide interest payments as fixed amounts (a stable income stream) but the value of the bond varies with the current interest rate.

- You can have stable income stream or stable principal value, but you cannot have them both.

A money market fund is an ideal place to park your money temporarily. It's lending your money with a day-to-day agreement regarding the interest rate. It's most like your bank savings account, except it is not FDIC insured. It's actually a special type of mutual fund that invests in very short-term high-quality securities. The returns on money market funds tend to be lower than other types of bond funds, and it differs in a more fundamental way.

You will learn that bonds are debt with very specific repayment terms. The interest payments (also called coupon payments) are fixed amounts at fixed times over longer periods. Consequently, the value of a bond, or bond fund, will change with current market interest rates.

In contrast, the value of a money market share is held at $1.00 per share. Your invested principal is stable but the interest rewarded to you as an investor changes with the market.

The key principal is that it is only possible to have fixed interest payments if the current market price fluctuates (e.g., bond funds), and that it is only possible to have fixed share price if the current interest rate moves with the market (e.g., money market funds).

The types of securities held by money market funds allow them to maintain a stable share price even during times of financial market stress. But they are not guaranteed; it is possible to lose money, although unlikely.

Use money market accounts like a bank account—a convenient place to park cash for short terms and to hold emergency funds. We will consider these "cash equivalents" and will not consider them for a long-term investment because they are unlikely to keep pace with inflation.

Lending vs. Owning—The Huge Bond Market

Stocks and bonds are both methods a company can use to raise money. Bonds are simple interest-only loans. Each has a specific term, usually one to thirty years, after which the principal is repaid. Everything is specified in a formal legal agreement called an *indenture*—which, unlike CDs or loans, makes a bond a *negotiable* instrument that can be bought or sold. If the worst happens, default, the bond holders get repaid in the bankruptcy proceedings before the stockholders get anything. The best that can happen is for the bondholders to get their principal back per the written agreement.

Stocks are ownership—forever. There are very few constraints, no bounds, no guarantees. Stocks are generally called "equity." Although the stock market often commands more media attention, the bond market is even bigger. It is vital to the ongoing operation of both the public and private sectors.

Bonds are issued to raise money for cities, states, the federal government and corporations. The primary and secondary bond markets are an essential part of the capital-raising process.

Bonds are bought and sold in huge quantities in the U.S. and around the world. Some bonds are easier to buy and sell than others—but that doesn't stop investors from trading all kinds of bonds virtually every second of every trading day.

Stable principal *or* stable interest payments—you can't have both. You may think that CDs might be an exception—and even more like a bank account because they are FDIC-insured. Learn some surprisingly interesting things about CDs in the next chapter.

Are CDs Better Than Bonds?

KEY CONCEPTS:

- Certificates of deposit (CDs) are bonds issued by banks or credit unions and insured by government agencies.

Sometimes CDs are better than bonds! Learn the rare advantage that small investors have over institutional investors in this episode.

A certificate of deposit (CD) offers a higher interest rate than a money market fund or a bank savings account but you don't have access to your money for a period of time without paying an early withdrawal fee. CDs offered by a bank or credit union are simple interest-only bonds that are sometime very attractive.

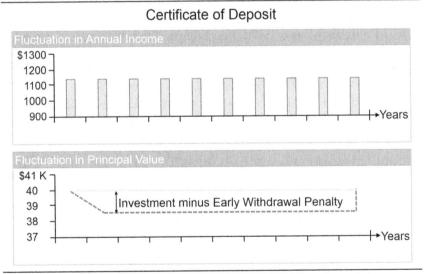

A CD from a bank or credit union is similar to a bond, but it cannot be traded on a secondary market so there is a penalty if not held to maturity. Sometimes there are attractive rates for small investors.

The highest paying CDs have higher yields than Treasury bonds and give the small investor a rare advantage over conventional bonds and brokered CDs. For instance, today the annual yield on a 5-year Treasury note is about one and a half percent. But, in contrast, the yield for CDs with equivalent term and risk varies from a high of

3% to nearly zero. Wow, that's quite a range, isn't it.[12]

When the 5-Year Treasury Note was 1.5%, the yield for federally-insured CDs (i.e. similar risk) varied from nearly zero to 3%.

CDs are like bonds in that they provide fixed monthly payments but cannot guarantee the full return of principal before the end of the term. The amount of the early withdrawal fee is limited: commonly 3 to 12 months of interest, depending on the bank or credit union.

While that's generally true, I've seen the early withdrawal fee waived for CDs in IRA accounts if you are over some age. I only mention this to emphasize the point that while the bond market is incredibly efficient, the CD market is not, and that creates some attractive opportunities for individual investors.

Are you familiar with CDs? Which of these would you say is true?

(1) Sometimes CDs are better investments than bonds.
(2) Large institutional investors invest in CDs.

Did you choose "institutional investors buy CDs"?

This is false. CDs are issued to individuals by banks or credit unions, and insured by federal agencies. So CDs—like U.S. Treasury Bonds—have essentially zero credit risk. But the FDIC or NCUA insurance levels are limited to amounts that make CDs attractive to individuals, but inappropriate for large institutional investors.

Did you choose "sometimes CDs are better"?

This is true. Keep in mind that bank CDs aren't negotiable—meaning, you can't sell them in any market. To redeem them, you must go back to the bank (or credit union) where you purchased them. But as I have shown, sometimes CDs are offered at above-market interest rates with low early-withdrawal fees.

If you can lock in a CD with a higher rate than the equivalent Treasury bond, then you obviously come out ahead for no additional credit risk. If interest rates go up, it can be even better!

I'll show you with a simple example. Here, you buy both a 4% CD and a 4% Treasury note—$1,000 for each. Towards the end of the first year, interest rates increase to 5% and you'd like to replace both to take advantage of the higher interest rates.

Example: Cost to Refinance (% of investment)

CD early withdrawal penalty:

$$= \frac{-4\% * 3 \text{ mo}}{12 \text{ mo}} = -1\%$$

Bond market price change:
$$= (\text{rate increase}) * (\text{duration})$$
$$= (4\% - 5\%) * 4 = -4\%$$

There is also a lot of variety in the early withdrawal penalties which can create attractive options if interest rates rise.

To sell your CD you will have to pay an early withdrawal penalty, which we'll say is 3 months interest for this example. Our annual interest rate divided by 12 is the interest rate per month, which we'd multiply by 3 months to get the early withdrawal penalty ($10). The penalty remains one percent of the amount of the CD for any day after that until the CD matures.

But an ordinary bond is different. There is no early withdrawal penalty, but its price changes every time the interest rates changes, and the amount the price changes gets smaller as the bond approaches maturity, or more precisely, as the bond duration approaches zero.

Remember, we bought this bond one year ago so there are now four years left on this bond. For now, let's say the duration is also equal to four years.

A bond price always changes in the opposite direction as interest rates by an amount equal to the rate change times the duration. So our simple estimate is that the cost to refinance the bond is four times more than the CD, or $40, which is our point. Sometimes, CDs are better than bonds.

Heads-up: there is also something called a "Brokered CD" and I cannot think of when they would be attractive—so tread carefully if your broker tries to sell you one.

Again, you're not going to get rich with bonds, but bonds are a critical element for controlling the level of risk in any portfolio, so it's vital that you understand the basics about how they work. Now if you understand how CDs work then you are well on your way to understanding how other bonds work—that's next!

What Are Bonds?

KEY CONCEPTS:

- Bonds are simple interest-only loans.

- Bond markets are extremely efficient.

- A bond's value (price) moves in opposite direction than interest rates—but not necessarily a bad thing for investors.

- Individual bonds and CDs return the face value at maturity—a uniquely valuable feature when the maturity date is matched with specific scheduled needs.

- On average, bonds do not appreciate in price like stocks do, but their prices do fluctuate over time.

- Using past returns for bond funds is particularly dangerous and usually misleading.

What are bonds? Bonds are simple interest-only loans. It's that simple! Learn what every investor should know about bonds and fixed-income securities.

Unlike buying a stock—where little is promised but the potential reward is unbounded—with a bond, everything is spelled out, and you don't get more than that. If we draw it as a picture, we're going to expect interest payments over regular periods but none of the principal is repaid until the end of the loan.

31

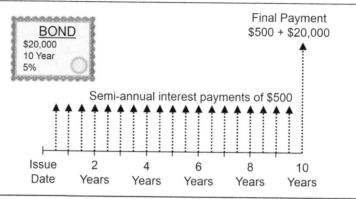

A simple bond is a commitment to a series of payments, like this.

When the borrower is a bank or credit union, these agreements are called certificates. When the borrower is a government or corporation, these are called bills, notes, or bonds, depending on the length of the loan. They have a face value—which is the amount you'll get back at the end of the term of the agreement, and a coupon which specifies the fixed dollar amount you'll receive every year as interest, in either monthly or semi-annual payments. Bonds with longer terms or poorer credit ratings need to offer higher coupons to attract investors.

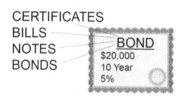

Fixed-income securities is the best general term that refers to all these types of securities.

The coupon rate never changes. That's the reason that bonds, like CDs, are called fixed-income investments. What makes these different from an IOU, a loan, or even a bank CD, is that these are "negotiable"—meaning you can buy and sell these in a market, for the current price.

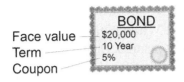

Face value — $20,000
Term — 10 Year
Coupon — 5%

Current Price: $19,976

The current value of any fixed income security varies with interest rates. This is worth repeating because it is often misunderstood.

It's a competitive market, and that price is determined by the prevailing interest rate for similar bonds. There is only one day that the price has to be equal to the face value of the bond, and that's its maturity date.

Interest rates move around daily. Today's interest rate for a 5-year Treasury note is around one and a half percent. At one point 30 years ago it was over fifteen percent.[13] Rates are determined by supply and demand in the market.

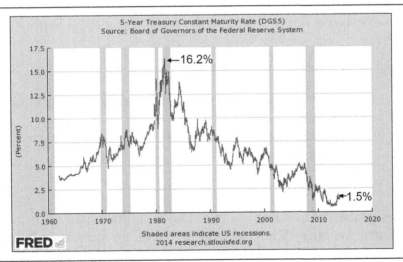

Interest rates can vary widely over time and also for the term length. But nobody can predict the future changes. Nobody!

The credit rating of the issuer is very important. Many corporations with outstanding credit ratings also issue bonds to raise money. Corporations with weaker credit ratings need higher coupons to attract investors, so these are called "high-yield bonds."

Now, as always, beware of marketing. While high-yield certificates are good, because they are government insured, high-yield bonds are bad—at least from our point of view that it's better to use high-quality bonds to stabilize your portfolio and keep your risk in your stock investments.[14] Because, in addition to default risk, junk bonds tend to go south when the stock market tanks, exactly the wrong time!

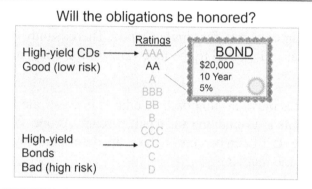

Will the obligations be honored?

Beware of marketing. A high-yield CD can have the lowest possible risk, whereas a high-yield bond is a high risk.

Think now. Which of these two facts is true?

(1) All bonds are subject to interest rate risk—unless held to maturity.
(2) Bonds prices vary with interest rates but do not grow like stock prices do.

Did you choose "unless held to maturity"?

This is false. Interest rate risk (also known as price risk) refers to the risk that the price of a bond will fall due to an increase in interest rates. There are no exceptions. When interest rates rise, and you have your money locked-up in a bond, you are missing out on investing that money at the new higher rate. The bond you own is instantly worth less from the amount of your lost opportunity. It's a lost opportunity even if you hold it to maturity and get each and every payment as promised, on time.

Did you choose "all bonds prices vary with interest rates"?

This is true. The market prices for bonds do not grow the way stock prices do, but their prices do fluctuate with interest rate changes.

The value of a stock reflects what people perceive the future profits will be for a company. So as a company grows, the value of the stock appreciates.

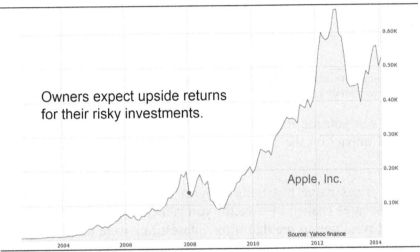

The price of stocks grow when profits grow. Not so with bonds!
A later chapter shows that speculating on individual stocks carries uncompensated risk.

Not so with bonds. A bond price, and the current interest rate, are directly connected, but the effect is not permanent.

To see this, consider a 5-year Treasury note. If interest rates never change, the market price for that bond would remain flat every day for five years.

But if interest rates went up 1% at the end of the first year the value is immediately worth a few percent less. Still, that Note will be worth exactly the face value on the very last day.

And if interest rates fall, the opposite occurs.

If interest rates fell an additional 1% every year for the life of the bond, the value of the bond might look like the following, where each fall in interest rates makes the bond more valuable. Intuitively this is what you'd expect, because your bond locked in higher interest rates than what's available in the market, but that ceases to have any additional value when the bond matures and is worth the face value.

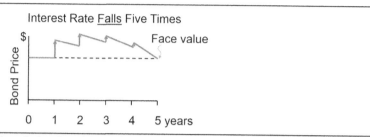

The value of a bond would rise if the interest rate fell 1% at the end of every year, but the impact diminishes as the duration decreases.

Now, can you see that the same size interest rate changes have a bigger impact on the bond price when the maturity date is further away?

Bond prices move instantaneously in the opposite direction when interest rates change by a factor you can control called "duration". Now I want you to see that if the interest rate were to instantly rise 1%, the price of a bond (or bond fund) with a 1-year duration would go down 1%. Down 1% causes a price rise of 1%. Longer-term bonds, and bonds with smaller interest payments, are more sensitive to interest rate changes because they have a longer duration. If the duration is 8 years, then a 1% change of interest rates causes the price to change by 8%.

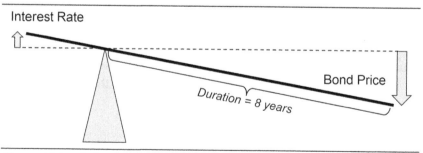

The sensitivity of a bond to interest rate changes increase with "duration", which is always shorter than the bond's "maturity".

The primary point is that a bond price isn't merely influenced by

36

interest rates, they are directly connected by math.

Another Story of Reducing Risk for Known Expenses

Life is unpredictable, and plans change. Young Buck had a rock solid job as a doctor, so he was comfortable putting 100% of his savings into the stock market. Then he got married and had twins. They needed that money for a down payment on a house. It was 2008. The stock market was in crisis and the financial news was dire. This reset their long-term savings back to zero.

On the other hand, Savvy Buck (his twin) invested the identical amount, but put 2/3 of that money into a stock market fund and the other 1/3 into CDs. To buy the identical home, Savvy sold his CDs plus $3,000 from stocks to come up with the $25,000 down payment. Further, he exchanged his remaining $9,000 in stocks for a balanced fund (comprised of 60% stocks and 40% bonds) which today (July 2014) has a value of $19,000 more than Young Buck, and the difference is growing exponentially. You can do this too! Use a bond with maturity matched to when money is needed to eliminate both stock market risks and from changing interest rates.

Savvy Buck was unusual in that he always knew that he wanted to buy a home in 2008. Most people can't anticipate their spending as accurately as Savvy. But he knew what he wanted, he knew that his money would be safer in CDs or bonds, and he knew he could even eliminate interest-rate risk. So, every time he put aside money towards this down payment, he purchased a CD that would mature in 2008. As the year 2008 approached, the duration of his CDs approached zero, making them insensitive to interest rate changes in the market.

We care about price sensitivity so we can invest in the appropriate type of bonds. We don't expect to get a return because of interest rate changes—because nobody can reliably predict interest rates. We're investors not speculators, so we're more concerned with total return which includes the dividends and reinvested dividends.

Next, we need to clear up the confusion about whether to buy individual bonds, bond funds, or bond ladders.

What is a Bond Ladder?

KEY CONCEPTS:

- Bond ladders are a collection of individual bonds; a self-managed fund.

- Use a single bond or a non-rolling ladder to automatically reduce interest rate risk as a date approaches.

- Use a rolling ladder to achieve the lowest possible fund expenses plus potential tax-loss harvesting.

At least two things are cool about individual bonds and bond ladders! Let first let me explain what a ladder is.

If you bought a ten-year bond every year for ten years we would call that a *ladder*. We give it that name because nine years in the future the first bond will have one year remaining, the second will have two years remaining, and so forth up to the last bond purchased which will have ten years remaining. The collection of maturities are like the rungs on a ladder.

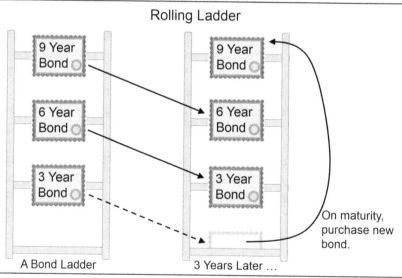

A rolling ladder is a self-managed bond fund where you buy new bonds as old bonds mature.

If new bonds are purchased as older bonds mature, you get a recurring, or rolling, ladder. A ladder may be comprised of any sort of bonds to effectively achieve a self-managed fund. In practice, it's only practical for CDs and U.S. Treasuries—because you can purchase these without a transaction cost or commission.

So if you have the time and discipline, you can build your own fund—and thereby avoid the expenses of a managed fund. That would be *one of two good reasons* to use individual bonds rather than a bond fund. But it's hard to beat the low cost of a good bond fund.

A *second good reason* to own individual bonds is a little less common, but it's exactly the strategy Savvy Buck used to purchase his house. In the last section we introduced the concept of "duration" as a measure of a bond's price sensitivity to a change in the interest rates.

A bond fund usually maintains a relatively constant duration. But both an individual bond or CD, and a non-rolling bond ladder, have a duration that decreases over time to zero. This means they become less sensitive to interest-rate changes as they approach maturity. That makes them perfect to fund a date-certain future liability. In fact, you could continue to buy them for that target date as I'm showing here. This collection of CDs or bonds is called a non-rolling ladder.

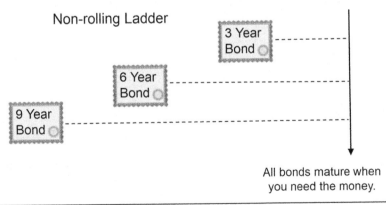

A non-rolling ladder is a way to minimize interest-rate risk by buying bonds that will mature when you will need the money.

It is usually possible to buy CDs, or Treasury Bonds when issued, without a fee. So a rolling ladder comprised of these would be a way to create a bond fund with the lowest possible annual expense.

However, stay away from other types of individual bonds. They often come with hefty fees of a few percent that are, unfortunately, not visible to ordinary investors.[15] You're usually better off buying a low-cost bond fund, and that's what we will talk about next.

Bond ladders are appropriate if you are willing to stay rather involved with your investments. Do you enjoy reading blogs and online discussions, like the Bogleheads forum? Then you have a good chance of knowing when and where there might be attractive CDs, or when TIPS (discussed later) might be attractive. Also, are you comfortable opening an account at a new online credit union, reading their fine print, and transferring your money to get their attractive CD rates? For you, owning individual bonds can be even better than owning low-cost bond mutual funds.

For the rest of us, it is easier to use low-cost bond mutual funds.

Individual Bonds or a Bond Fund?

KEY CONCEPTS:

- A bond fund is identical in both performance and risk to a rolling bond ladder with the same duration.

- Low-cost is key.

- For savvy investors, sometimes individual bonds or CDs are the best opportunities.

- Bond mutual funds provide liquidity, are convenient, and many are both excellent and low cost.

- Electronically Traded Funds (ETFs) are similar to mutual funds but traded like stocks. They are useful for investors who want to be slightly more involved.

Should you own individual bonds or a bond fund? For most of us, a bond fund is the easy answer. The major factors in deciding whether to use a bond fund come down to convenience, costs, and control over maturity.

That said, here are five instances when individual bonds and CDs can be more attractive than bond funds.

1. Expenses. You don't need much diversification if you use CDs and US Treasuries, and you can own these with no purchase fees or annual expenses.

Other individual bonds, on the other hand, can have spreads between the bid price and the asking price from 0.5% up to 5.0%, and you will, unfortunately, have no idea that you are paying these hefty fees to your broker.[16]

A bond fund is more convenient than buying individual securities. Bond mutual funds are just like stock mutual funds in that you put your money into a pool with other investors to be invested professionally. This can be done at a very low cost.

2. Opportunities. For various reasons CDs are sometimes available with well above market yields. Similarly, the inflation-adjusted return from owning TIPS (discussed later) varies and savvy investors opportunistically buy when these real returns are up.

3. Matching bond maturity to a date-specific need guarantees you can meet that need despite any interest rate changes.

Two additional reasons why individual bonds are sometimes better than bond funds *in taxable accounts* are worth mentioning:

4. Tax-loss harvesting, and

5. State-specific tax costs (e.g., municipal bonds from other states).

But, aren't individual bonds safer than bond funds? No! What some people find confusing is that generally bond funds never mature. So while there's not a specific date when they'll return what you invested, the fund has a price and you can sell it at any time.

Remember, we don't expect this price to appreciate, like we would with the stock of a growing company. We care about the *total return*, which we'll talk more about later, and sometimes we care about how sensitive that price is to interest rate changes. That sensitivity is best expressed by its duration. A short-term bond fund is less sensitive to interest rate changes than a long-term bond fund.

Your last challenge question is an easy one. Which of these is true?

> (1) An interest rate increase can be good for investors.
> (2) A bond fund is just as risky as a stock fund.

Did you choose "risky as a stock fund"?

This is false. First of all, a terrible year in the stock market is when the value of your investments drops forty to fifty percent. Whereas a terrible year in the bond market might be if interest rates suddenly jump a few percent causing the value of all bonds to drop. Hang on though, if you chose a bond or bond fund that you'll hold for longer than its duration, then rising interest rates are actually your friend.

Did you choose "interest rate increase can be good"?

This is true. If you reinvest dividends at the new higher interest rate, then you come out ahead if you hold bonds for longer than their duration. Let me use an example to illustrate this.

This investor buys a 30-year 5% Treasury bond at par, and seconds after it is issued, yields suddenly rise to 10%. This bond is now worth less than 53 cents on the dollar. However, since this bond throws off coupons which can be reinvested at the new higher yield, it takes our investor less than 11 years to break even—so this defines the bond's duration. And note that—because of the coupons—the duration is always less than the maturity, sometimes considerably so. To reiterate, after 11 years, this investor is better off for the fall in price because of the rise in yield.

Key point: The duration is the period of time at which you are indifferent to interest rate changes.[17]

Typically, when you invest in a bond mutual fund, they keep investing in new bonds such that the duration of the fund remains fairly stable. Such a bond mutual fund is similar in both performance and risk to a rolling bond ladder with the same duration.

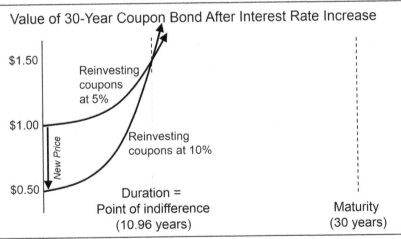

Value of 30-Year Coupon Bond After Interest Rate Increase

Interest rate increases benefit investors that hold them for longer than the "duration" and reinvest the dividends at the new rate.

Joe thinks he understands *duration* now, and finds a low-cost Long-Term Treasury Bond fund that lists its duration as eleven years.

Even though it is a fund, rather than an individual Treasury bond like in the last example, Joe figures if interest rates were to increase any amount, he wouldn't care about that change if he owns it for another eleven years longer and reinvest the interest coupons at the new rate. Is he right? ... Yes!

Mutual funds not only provide professional management but superb liquidity and very low-cost. As always, **low-cost is key**.

There are hundreds of funds to choose from. How do you recognize a good one? That's next. But first, let's recap what we've learned so far.

RECAP

Bonds are essential to every investment portfolio—even when yields are at record low levels—because stocks are so risky. Owning the right amount of bonds helps make that stock market risk palatable. They're the perfect investment when you need money at a specific time. And bonds that are uncorrelated with the stock market are a very attractive diversifier.

Stocks and bonds are the two most important asset classes. A smart investor gets this allocation right. People that talk about three major asset classes are merely recognizing the importance to diversify stocks, and consider U.S. stocks separately than International stocks.

Stocks, bonds, and money market funds are each very different, and we took a look at this to introduce this current series about bonds. CDs are a special type of bond, and we looked at how and why, sometimes, CDs are better than bonds.

Then we talked about bonds and their two major attributes: the quality (or credit rating) of the issuer, and the time-to-maturity of the bond. We saw how a bond price is tied to the interest rate, and introduced the concept of "duration" to describe price sensitivity.

Bond price and yield are mathematically tied to each other—when one rises, the other falls—but the periodic payments (also called "coupon" payments) remains the same.

It is easy to buy CDs and individual bonds from your bank or broker and make a bond ladder. This is interesting for the lowest possible annual expenses, and when you want them to mature on a specific date for some reason.

Low cost is the way to go. This can be achieved with both individual Treasury bonds and CDs, or with low-cost bond funds.

We looked at how duration helps us decide between short-, intermediate-, and long-term bond funds.

All bonds are subject to interest rate risk. All bonds are subject to interest rate risk. All bonds are subject to interest rate risk. All bonds are subject to interest rate risk. All bonds are subject to interest rate risk. All bonds are subject to interest rate risk. All bonds are subject to interest rate risk. All bonds are subject to interest rate risk. **All bonds are subject to interest rate risk.** All bonds are subject to interest rate risk. All bonds are subject to interest rate risk. All bonds are subject to interest rate risk. All bonds are subject to interest rate risk. All bonds are subject to interest rate risk. All bonds are subject to interest rate risk. All bonds are subject to interest rate risk. All bonds are subject to interest rate risk. All bonds are subject to interest rate risk. All bonds are subject to interest rate risk. All bonds are subject to interest rate risk. All bonds are subject to interest rate risk. All bonds are subject to interest rate risk. All bonds are subject to interest rate risk. All bonds are subject to interest rate risk. <u>All bonds</u>

This is often misunderstood. There are no exceptions. All bonds are subject to interest rate risk—whether insured, AAA, or guaranteed—all certificates of deposit, all individual bonds, and all bond funds.

Bonds: Risks and Returns

Nearly all the risk from owning bonds is driven by two factors: the *time to maturity* and the *credit quality of the issuer*. This chapter explores these two, plus mentions others to be aware of, so you can understand what bond investments are appropriate for your portfolio.

A simple map of investment possibilities might look like this 9-box style guide. For most investors, the role of bonds is to add safety and anchor your portfolio during falling stock markets ("bear" markets), allowing you to stay disciplined. We will discuss why short- and intermediate-term low-cost bond funds comprised of the highest grade bonds satisfy your needs. There are also times when locking in high interest rates with longer-term CD, individual bonds, or especially TIPS can be valuable. And just as important: why you should avoid lower-quality bonds and more expensive actively-managed bond funds.

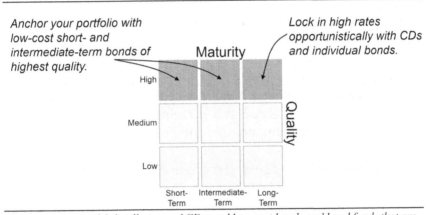

Experts recommend federally-insured CDs, and low-cost bonds and bond funds that are high-quality to keep your risk isolated to your stock holdings.

Yield, Price And Making Comparisons

KEY CONCEPTS:

- Yield-To-Maturity (YTM) is the best way to compare *individual* bonds.

- 30-day SEC Yield is best way to compare bond *funds*.

- *Total return* is the best way to measure and compare the performance of any investments, of any types.

This chapter will clarify the key metrics to compare bonds and bond funds, the importance of *total return* for measuring performance, the usefulness of *duration* for controlling interest rate risk, and some practical insights we can infer about the market's expectations for the future as revealed by current pricing (*yield curves*).

How To Compare Individual Bond Returns

The word *yield* is used in multiple descriptive phrases but three are the most important: coupon yield, current yield and yield to maturity. Each has a very precise meaning. Let's look at each.

Coupon yield is set when a bond is issued. It is the interest rate paid by the bond, and it is listed as a percentage of par, or face value, which is the principal amount that will be paid at maturity.

The *coupon yield* designates a fixed dollar amount that never changes through the life of the bond. If a $1,000 par value bond is described as having a 10% coupon, that coupon will always be $100 for each bond, paid out in $50 increments every six month for the entire life of the bond—no matter what happens to the price of the bond, or to interest rates. That is the reason bonds are called fixed-income securities.

Current yield. Almost as soon as a bond starts trading in the secondary market, it ceases to trade at par. A bond's *current yield* is its annual coupon divided by its market price.

Example: Say a bond has a face value of $20,000 and makes annual interest payments of $1,200. You buy it at 90, meaning that you pay 90% of the face value, or $18,000. It is five years from maturity. The bond's *current yield* is 6.7%:

($1,200 annual interest / $18,000 x 100) = 6.7%

While current yield is easy to calculate, it is not as accurate a measure as yield to maturity. See in the next example why the yield to maturity for this same bond is 8.54%.

Yield to Maturity, sometimes called the bond's *yield* for short.

You can see from the above description that current yield is based only on the coupon and the current market price. Current yield fails to measure two important sources of income that investors earn from bonds: compound interest—from reinvesting (not spending) the coupon payments—and changes in the bond price.

Yield to maturity (YTM) is a more comprehensive measure of potential return than "current yield" and it is the most valuable measure for comparing individual bonds. It estimates the total amount that a bond will earn over the entire life of an individual bond, from all possible sources of income—coupon income, interest-on-interest, and capital gains or losses due to the difference between the price paid when the bond was purchased and par, the return of principal at maturity. The next example and picture will illustrate this.

Example: In the previous example we calculated that bond's *current yield* is 6.7%. But the bond's *yield to maturity* in this case is higher. It considers that you can achieve compounding interest by reinvesting the $1,200 you receive each year. It also considers that when the bond matures, you will receive $20,000, which is $2,000 more than what you paid. The next picture shows that each future payment is discounted to what it is worth today. The YTM is 8.54%, or the discount rate such that the values of all future payments sum to the current market price.

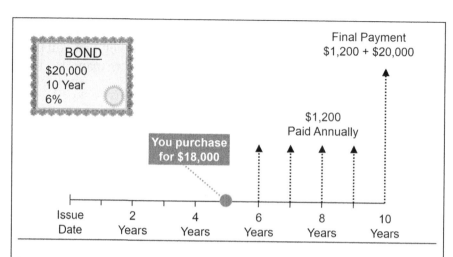

Pricing The Bond With Yield of 8.54%

In this example, the market establishes the *yield* for 5-year maturities (the amount remaining on our 10-year bond) at 8.54%. Each future coupon is discounted by dividing by (1+YTM) for each year. We can see that the current bond price is exactly the present value of future coupons and return of face value at maturity:

Year 6 coupon	$1200 / 1.0854 =	$	1,106
Year 7 coupon	$1200 / (1.0854)^2 =	$	1,019
Year 8 coupon	$1200 / (1.0854)^3 =	$	938
Year 9 coupon	$1200 / (1.0854)^4 =	$	865
Year 10 coupon	$1200 / (1.0854)^5 =	$	797
Year 10 face value	$20,000 / (1.0854)^5 =	$	13,276
	Current value of bond at 8.54% =	$	18,000

The *yield to maturity* will give you an estimate of the *total return* of the bond, assuming the bond is held to maturity and all coupons are reinvested at a rate equal to the yield to maturity.

Key Point: The chief usefulness of YTM quotes is that they allow you to compare different kinds of bonds—those with dissimilar coupons, different market prices relative to par (for instance, bonds selling at premiums or discounts), and different maturities.

How to Compare Bond Fund Returns

Unlike individual bonds, since there is no single date at which the entire portfolio of a *bond fund* matures, *bond funds* cannot quote a YTM equivalent to that of individual bonds.

Indeed, most bond funds maintain what is known as a constant maturity. That means, for example, that if a bond fund invests in long-term bonds, then bonds are bought and sold continually to maintain a portfolio long-term maturity of ten years or greater.

SEC Yield. Yield of a bond fund measures the income received from the underlying bonds held by the fund. The 30-day annualized yield is a standard formula for all bond funds based on the yields of the bonds in the bond fund, averaged over the past 30 days. This figure shows you the yield characteristics of the fund's investments at the end of the 30-day period. It does not indicate the fund's future yield. The 30-day yield also helps you compare bond funds from different companies on a standard basis.

The chief value of the 30-day SEC Yield is to compare various types of bond funds. Think of the SEC yield as the average YTM of the fund for a recent 30-day period.

The price of a bond fund changes continually in response to changes in interest rates—exactly as with individual bonds (because that's what it's a collection of!). As a result, the price of any bond fund at any future date is impossible to predict, but it doesn't vary any differently than the individual bonds of which it is comprised.

Returns posted by bond funds for prior periods, and listed in daily newspapers, are *total returns*. They always include changes in the price of the bond fund due to changes in interest rates. This is always the best way to measure and compare past performance of any bonds or bond funds. In the next chapter we will learn how to use duration to reduce risk from changing interest rates.

Don't be tempted to compare funds based on other numbers that might look attractive. For instance, *Distribution Yields*, which are sometimes computed from the prior year's distributions. These are particularly misleading because they reflect interest rate changes and capital distributions. Instead use *Yield-To-Maturity* to compare individual bonds, use *30-day SEC Yield* to compare bond funds, or use *total return* to compare anything with anything.

Total Return—To Measure And Compare Performance

Total return. A bond fund's *total return* measures its overall gain or loss over a specific period of time. *Total return* includes income generated by the underlying bonds and (both realized and unrealized) price gains or losses. Investors should focus on total return when evaluating performance of bond funds.

Investors in fixed-income securities sometimes make the mistake of equating interest income or advertised yield with return. But this does not take into consideration what is happening to principal.

Total return for bonds consists of whatever you earn in interest income, plus or minus changes in the value of principal. (To be totally accurate, you would also subtract taxes and commission expenses from return.)

Example: Let's assume that a year ago, you invested $10,000 in a bond fund, purchasing 1,000 shares at $10.00 each. Assume also that the bond fund was advertising a yield of 10%, or $1.00 per share, which was maintained for the entire year. But suppose that in the meantime, interest rates have risen so that now bond funds with similar maturity and credit quality yield 11%. As a result, your bond fund is now selling for $9.00 per share. What is the *total return* on that investment for the past year?

You have earned interest income (based on the monthly coupon distributions) of 10%, or $1,000. But, that ignores the fact that your bond fund has now lost approximately $1 per share (10% of its principal value) and that your principal is now worth $9,000.

Add the income earnings of $1,000 to the current value of your fund ($9,000). Your investment is now worth $10,000. (For the sake of simplicity, I am ignoring interest-on-interest and commission costs.) Therefore, the net return is $0, or 0%. That is your total return, to date, even though you have received 10% interest income.

If instead interest rates had declined to 9%, the price of your bond fund would have risen to $11,000, and your capital gains would have added to the interest income your fund distributed, and your total return would have risen to 20%:

($1,000 interest + $1,000 price increase)/$10,000 = 20%

The concept of *total return* applies equally to individual stocks and bonds and to funds of every kind.

Total return is ultimately what we care about—and we want this to be larger than inflation. And the beauty is that it gives us a way to compare any of your investments with any others.

For both stock and bond funds, *total return* over time is conveniently depicted by a chart that is called *Growth of Hypothetical $10,000.* This is the fair way to compare funds comprised of different types of assets.

Example: Comparing Total Returns

Growth of Hypothetical $10,000

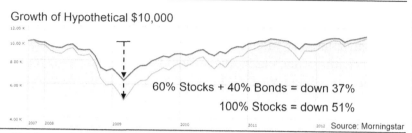

60% Stocks + 40% Bonds = down 37%

100% Stocks = down 51%

Source: Morningstar

Use "total return" to compare funds that have different mixtures of assets. Usually this is published in charts like this titled "Growth of Hypothetical $10,000".

Suppose you wanted to consider how two portfolios[18] with different asset allocations fared over the great recession in 2008-2010. You would do this by comparing total returns, which is most easily accessed in charts titled *Growth of Hypothetical $10,000*. The 100% stock portfolio lost more than 51% from its peak in 2007 whereas the 60/40 portfolio lost 37% over the same period. If withdrawals were required and recovery took a decade, the safety in the balanced portfolio is apparent. As it turned out, the stock market rebounded relatively quickly this time and so long-term stock investors escaped scot-free this time—except for those that panicked and abandoned their plans. Remember, a very important reason to own a balanced portfolio is to give you the emotional fortitude to "Stay the Course".

Remember, when comparing bond funds, look at *total return* (also called Growth of $10,000) and the *30-day SEC Yield*.

High-quality bond investors have fared well 2008-2012, both because interest rates dropped as the Federal Reserve tried to stimulate the economy and from a flight to quality that accompanied the uncertainty. But since interest rates can change in both directions it is important that we learn how to reduce risk from interest rate changes for when we need to.

How To Reduce Risk From Interest Rate Changes

KEY CONCEPTS:

- *Duration* is an essential attribute for understanding the riskiness of a bond fund or ladder over time.

- The *duration* of a bond, or a bond fund, is a measure of its price sensitivity to interest rate changes.

- Investors are indifferent to interest-rate changes if they hold their bond (or bond fund) for the length of time called *duration* after interest rates change.

- Individual bonds have declining *duration*. (This is useful.)

- Bond funds have constant *duration*. (This is also useful.)

We've learned that all bonds and bond funds are subject to interest rate risk—that is: if rates go up, the bond prices instantly go down, preserving the time value of money.

Bond *maturity* provides a rough indication of 'riskiness'. All other things being equal, the longer the time period to maturity for each bond, the greater the volatility of its price. However, this measure only takes into account the final payment (not any other cash flows), does not take into account the time value of money and therefore does not give an accurate comparison of relative 'riskiness' across bonds.[19]

Heads-up! I'm going to teach you a new word. It's valuable, useful, and worth knowing. But, you are going to trip because your brain already thinks it knows this word. It will help if every time I write *duration*, you mentally replace it with the words *"financial duration"*. Then you'll remember it is special, and you'll be fine.

Duration is a better factor to characterize risk than *time to maturity*. It's a more sophisticated measure as it takes into account all cash flows and time value of money. It tells how long you'd have to hold a bond or bond fund after an interest rate change to be indifferent to such changes. After demonstrating this, you'll learn how to use duration to compare riskiness across bonds and estimate the impact of an interest rate change.

Duration: The Point of Indifference to Interest Rates

The <u>first</u> valuable way that the duration of a bond or bond fund can be applied is to reduce interest rate risk by matching duration to the point in time of specific liabilities. I'll walk you through this. William J. Bernstein offers a valuable definition[20]:

> Duration is *the point at which you become indifferent to changes in price and yield.*

Mr. Bernstein provides this example to illustrate the first important concept of finding the point in the future where you become indifferent to an interest rate change today. Consider a one-year Treasury bill. A bill is in reality a zero coupon bond. It is bought at a discount with no interest payments before maturity. For example, a 5% bill will sell for $0.9524 ($1.00/1.05) and be redeemed at par ($1.00). If someone purchases this 5% bill, and a few seconds after it is issued yields suddenly rise to 10%, it falls in price to $0.9091 ($1.00/1.10), with an immediate loss of 4.55%.

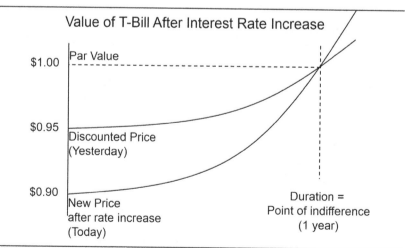

CDs, bonds, and bond funds each have a "duration". This is the length of time it would take for an investor to become indifferent to an interest rate increase. Holding longer, the investor would come out ahead. Holding shorter, the investor loses.

But, if our investor holds the bill to maturity, he will receive the full 5% return, the same as if there had been no yield rise/price fall. And beyond the one year maturity, it's all gravy—our investor can now reinvest the entire proceeds at double the yield. His "point of indifference" is thus the one-year maturity of the bill; before one year he is worse off because of the yield rise/price fall, and after one year he is better off.[21]

The formula for bond duration is complex, but the most important thing to remember is that the bigger the coupon or yield, the larger the gap between duration and maturity—at 10% yields a bond with 10 years maturity will have a much shorter duration than at a yield of 5%. And finally, for a zero-coupon bond, maturity and duration are the same.[22]

Duration tells us how long we must wait to become indifferent to an interest-rate change. The following two sidebars will help you get an intuitive grasp of how this important concept of *duration* is related to *coupons* and *maturity*. The way these interact with each other becomes apparent if you were to consider balancing them on a teeter-totter.

Duration of a Zero Coupon Bond is equal to its time to maturity.

The lever above represents the five-year time period it takes for this zero-coupon bond to mature. The money balancing on the far right represents the present value of the amount that will be paid to the bondholder at maturity. The fulcrum, or the point balancing the lever, represents *duration*, which must be positioned where the lever is balanced. The fulcrum balances the lever at the point on the time line at which 50% of the cash flows (on a net present value basis) will have been returned. The entire cash flow of a zero-coupon bond occurs at maturity, so the fulcrum is located directly below this one payment.[23]

This extreme case, where the coupons are $0.00, shows that small coupons don't have much effect on making duration less than the time to maturity. Next, we see that bigger interest payments do.

Duration of a Simple Coupon Bond is always less than its time to maturity. [24]

Consider a simple bond that pays coupons annually and matures in ten years. Its cash flows consist of ten annual coupon payments and the last payment includes the face value of the bond.

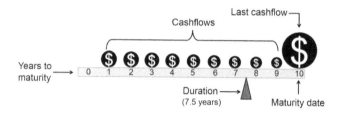

The money represents the present value of all cash flows you will receive over the ten-year period. Their sum equals the amount paid for the bond. The fulcrum balances the lever at the point on the time line at which 50% of the cash flows (on a net present value basis) will have been returned. The picture above shows the duration of this bond is 7.5 years.

As coupons are distributed and the present value of remaining cash flows are recalculated, the timeline to bond maturity gets shorter and the fulcrum shifts to the right. CDs and individual bonds all have declining duration as time approaches the bond maturity.

This picture provides an intuitive way to grasp why the coupon payments don't do much to shorten the duration when the bond gets close to maturity.

Regular coupon bonds make coupon payments throughout its life, as do a collection of bonds—be they in a bond ladder or in a huge fund. Very often the term *average duration* is specified to characterize the entire collection. The point of indifference to interest rate changes applies identically for a fund as for individual bonds. A characteristic of funds is that they are often managed to maintain a collection of bonds that produce a rather stable, or constant, average duration.

Key Point: Individual bonds have declining duration that ultimately becomes zero when the bond matures.

A zero-coupon bond automatically reduces duration by exactly the amount of time that passes, and is therefore the risk-less choice for meeting a future obligation. A coupon-paying bond approximates this: duration declines very slowly at first and then more rapidly once the bond nears its maturity; this is more pronounced when interest rates are high and less important when rates are low.

A bond fund duration is relatively constant.[25] For most purposes, it is easy to gradually shift from intermediate- or longer-term bonds to shorter-term bonds as the need for capital approaches, which will reduce sensitivity to interest-rate changes.

Duration: The Measure of Sensitivity to Interest Rates

To be absolutely assured of receiving a given sum on a future date, your goal is to gradually reduce the sensitivity to interest rate increases as the date approaches. The financial term "duration" is also a measure of this sensitivity. The significance of a declining duration is the declining sensitivity to interest rate changes.

The <u>second</u> valuable application of duration is for a quick estimate of just how much the price of a bond or bond fund would immediately change after a small change in interest rates. I'll call it a rule-of-thumb to give it an appropriate context.

Bond Price Change (%) = - (interest rate change in %) x duration

An example mentioned earlier is that a bond with a 5-year duration will decrease 5% in price with each 1% increase in yield. The same would be true for an intermediate-term bond fund that has a 5-year duration.

Limitations: If you use this as a rule-of-thumb to help you make comparisons you will be making good decisions. If you are expecting precision, you'll be disappointed.

For one reason, this second application of duration uses a slightly different definition for duration. Secondly, this *modified definition* is only valid for small changes in interest rates. Historically, rate changes have been rather gradual—so that hasn't been a problem.

Lastly, it's not entirely clear how each fund computes duration. For instance, both Fidelity and Vanguard call it 'Average Duration', but to define it Fidelity seems to use the time-weighted definition and Vanguard seems to use the ratio definition. In truth, they may both use something different to handle the bonds that have special features like call provisions. My advice: use it then move on! Use it as a rough metric to make good decisions and then move on with your life. Duration is a valuable tool! But if you are using it to manage a corporate pension fund then you would be reading an advanced book.

The earlier example where a hapless investor experienced the one-time *instantaneous* 5% interest-rate increase was useful to illustrate important point that you can be indifferent to interest rate if you hold the bond for the duration and reinvest the dividends at the new rates. Past history suggests that rates change at a much more gradual rate. This next side bar shows interest rates gradually increasing over 4% over a two year period, and the total returns of all bonds continued to grow.

Example: The Federal Reserve influences interest rates by controlling the very short-term Federal Funds rate. Changes are very gradual. For example they increased from 1% to 5.2% at a steady gradual pace over two years (mid-2004 to mid-2006). Yes, the bond prices responded exactly as I have described—bond pricing is mostly simple math, not emotions or projections—but the loss in bond values from rising rates simply made the total returns less positive. The following chart shows the *total return* of $10,000 invested in short-, intermediate-, and long-term U.S. Treasury bond index funds—continuing to grow, just slower:

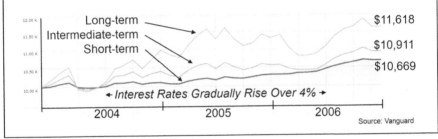

Another important lesson from history is that nobody can predict interest rates. There are currently a lot of people that think rates are so low that there is nowhere to move but up. They have thought this for six years now. And if they have stayed in short-term bonds because of this reasoning they have already lost several years of the higher yields from, say, intermediate-term bonds. Nobody knows how low this, or any, interest rate environment will last. But you can become indifferent to changes! Hold short or intermediate-term high-quality bonds based on when you need the money—avoid speculating on future interest rate changes.

Since we are investors, not speculators (gamblers), we also don't want to gamble on future rates of inflation. You cannot predict this! Nobody can. But we can own bonds in a way that protects us if inflation is higher than expected, and also if inflation is lower than expected.

How To Reduce Risk From Unexpected Inflation

KEY CONCEPTS

- *TIPS* are special bonds where the principal adjusts with the consumer price index; TIPS investors win if inflation is higher than expected

- The market establishes interest rates for every maturity. The result is a *yield curve* for a set of similar securities (e.g., the U.S. Treasury Yield Curve)

- In the end, we care about *real* (inflation adjusted) growth

- *Nominal* interest rates includes market's best estimate of future inflation; investors win if actual inflation is lower

Inflation is a big risk. Long-term investments in stocks produce growth significantly above inflation, but what about portfolios that have a significant percentage of bonds?

Many choose Treasury Inflation Protected Securities (TIPS) for protection against unexpectedly high inflation. While these are issued with a lower coupon rate, don't misunderstand this, because both the principal and interest of TIPS are indexed to inflation. So, if inflation increases by 0.2% one month, then the principal of this special type of bond increases by 0.2%, and the coupon interest rate is applied to the new inflation-adjusted principal. As a result, if there is 3% inflation every year for ten years, a $1,000 TIPS will return $1,344 (=1000*(1.03)^{10})to the bond holder when it matures, rather than $1,000 as would a normal Treasury bond. The purchasing power of the invested principal will be the same as the $1,000 had ten years earlier, it's just that the principal money has been adjusted for inflation.

That's it! You can skip ahead to the next chapter now about how to build your portfolio. Or, read on to learn more about how it works.

Real versus Nominal Interest Rates

Learning more is easy, but I need to teach you another word. All through this book we have talked about interest rates but now we need to be more precise. They were actually nominal interest rates.

Nominal interest rates are not inflation adjusted.

Real interest rates have inflation subtracted out from them.

Ultimately, we all seek to grow the purchasing power of our money after inflation. The coupons for Treasury Inflation Protected Securities (TIPS) are smaller and represent this real interest rate because the principal amount of these securities grow with the Consumer Price Index[26]. The *real* interest rate is just that—the rate of interest an investment earns that is above inflation. The *nominal* interest rate that we have discussed so far is comprised of the inflation rate plus the real interest rate[27].

Nominal = Real Interest Rate + Breakeven Inflation Rate

Our goal is to protect ourselves from inflation. We will identify strategies to protect our investments both if inflation is higher than expected, and if inflation is lower than expected. First we have to return to our friend, the yield curve. We are now in a position to discuss the determinants of a bond's yield. As we will see, the yield on any particular bond is a reflection of a variety of factors, some common to all bonds and some specific to the issue under consideration.

The Valuable Meaning in a Yield Curve

I'm going to introduce this to you, not because you need to interpret yield curves (you don't), but because this will help you to understand the relationship between interest rates and expected inflation.

A yield curve is a graph demonstrating the relationship between yield and maturity for a set of similar securities. A number of yield curves are available, but the one that investors compare all others to is the U.S. Treasury Yield Curve.

At any point in time, short-term and long-term interest rates will generally be different. Sometimes short-term rates are higher, sometimes lower. Each day, in addition to a table of Treasury prices and yields, a plot of the yield curve for U.S. Treasuries is published at treasury.gov.[28]

These yield curves change over time. The Federal Reserve's policy drives the yields for short maturities. All other rates (longer maturities) are set by the market.

In this example, the *nominal* interest rate curve represents the current yields for U.S. Treasuries of each maturity. The curve beneath this are the current yields for Treasury Inflation Protected Securities (TIPS) of each maturity. The difference between them represents the *Breakeven Inflation Rate*.

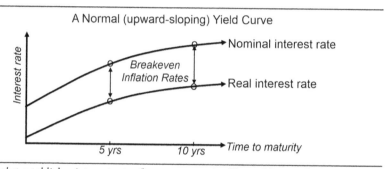

The market establishes interest rates for every maturity. The yield curve for TIPS is the nominal interest rate on U.S. Treasuries minus expected inflation rate for every maturity.

Breakeven Inflation Rate is mostly the expected inflation that is built into Treasury interest rates. If inflation is less than expected, then investors that buy Treasuries come out ahead. If inflation is more than expected, then investors that buy TIPS come out ahead. The Breakeven Inflation Rate is actually slightly bigger than expected inflation because it also included a small premium being the cost investors are willing to pay to guarantee real returns.

This composite yield curve is hypothetical to illustrate the key concepts in a simple way. It would look different if inflation is expected to fall. Additionally, expected future real rates could be larger or smaller than the current real rate.

In 2012, all Treasuries with less than 20-year maturities were yielding less than inflation. Investors are *paying* a premium for safety when they invest in these securities. While unusual, this price for safety is not a good reason to abandon your investment plan and accept a higher level of risk than you accepted before.

That means that the corresponding *real* interest rates were negative! Why would you invest in a bond with negative yield? This does not mean that an investor will experience negative returns. Read on ...

Why Include TIPS In Your Portfolio?

TIPS are like traditional Treasury bonds but offer insurance against inflation in a different manner. At each semi-annual coupon payment, the principal value of the bond receives an adjustment based on the current rate of inflation. Future interest payments are computed from the new inflation-adjusted bond value.

Traditional Bonds are a better investment if future inflation is less than expected, and TIPS are a better investment if future inflation is greater than expected. But there is more.

With a normal yield curve, investors can earn higher interest rates if they accept the risks associated with longer-term bonds—and that includes unexpected inflation.

Key Point: The *biggest* advantage of TIPS is that investors can earn that term premium without taking the risk of unexpected inflation.

TIPS have only been in existence since 1997, but long enough for bond expert Larry Swedroe to assert that TIPS are even slightly negatively correlated with the stock market (i.e. better than traditional Treasuries). This means a smaller amount of TIPS can achieve an investor's risk position, enabling a bigger investment in the stock market for higher expected return.

Consider this: can you determine, based on these numbers, which is the better investment?

10-year Treasury bond yielding 2%, or
10-year TIPS yielding -0.5% (yes, that's negative 0.5%)

No. You don't know and you can't know at the time you purchase the bond. That's because the yield of the TIPS does not include the inflation adjustment that will be applied monthly to the price of the TIPS. It may be higher than 2% or lower, depending on the future inflation rate.

But these yields do tell us what the market expects will be the Breakeven Inflation Rate:

Breakeven inflation rate = YTM(traditional) − YTM(TIPS) = 2.5%

Key point: The breakeven rate is defined as the rate that would result in equivalent total returns for both types of bonds.

The expected return for the traditional Treasury bond is simply the yield to maturity (on the *nominal* curve). For TIPS, the expected return is the yield to maturity (on the *real* curve) plus the expected inflation adjustments. Notice that the expected returns between the two bonds are the same![29]

If the rate of inflation turns out to be higher than 2.5%, then due to the inflation adjustment, the TIPS will turn out to have been the better buy. But if the rate of inflation is lower than 2.5%, then because of higher interest payments during the life of the conventional T-bond, that will turn out to have been the better buy.

In this first scenario we see how the TIPS bond is the better buy when actual inflation turns out to be higher than expected:

Actual Inflation = 3.5% (higher than originally expected 2.5%)		
	Treasury bond	**TIPS bond**
Yield to Maturity	2.00%	-0.50%
Inflation Adjustment	(none)	3.50%
Actual Return	2.00%	3.00%

In this next scenario we see that when actual inflation is lower than expected, then traditional bonds do better.

Actual Inflation = 1.5% (less than originally expected 2.5%)		
	Treasury bond	**TIPS bond**
Yield to Maturity	2.00%	-0.50%
Inflation Adjustment	(none)	1.50%
Actual Return	2.00%	1.00%

A strategy many investors use to protect themselves from inflation being different than expected (because nobody can predict the future), is to purchase half (or more) of their bonds as TIPS.

Key Point: The difference between the yield of a Treasury bond and a TIPS with the same maturity reflects the market's expectation of inflation for the period.

Key Point: The market's expectations for inflation is built into the rates. If inflation turns out to be *less* than expected, investors come out ahead. And if inflation is greater than expected, investors do better with TIPS.

Key Point: There is not a single interest rate and the government does not set interest rates. Rather, the U.S. federal government sets Federal Funds rate and the market determines these yield curves based on their expectations about inflation and prospects for the future.

Key Point: A bond rides the yield curve for its entire life. It might be originally issued as a 20-year security, but after ten years it gets priced like it is a 10-year bond (because it is one now). And as it approaches maturity, the yield on it falls to essentially money market yields. Bond funds rarely hold bonds all the way to maturity.

Key Point: There are sweet spots on the Yield Curve. Investors might get a 0.1% per year increase in yield for extending maturity in the very short-term. Returns might increase 0.3% per year for extending maturity for years 4 through 10, and then decrease to only 0.1% per year for extending longer.

Bond expert Larry Swedroe has suggested a rule-of-thumb of choosing: select the longer maturity if the return is at least 0.2% per year for nominal bonds (or 0.15% per year for municipal bonds).[30]

Lastly, taxation matters, and issues can be avoided by holding TIPS as mutual funds, or holding individual TIPS in a tax-advantaged account.

To summarize, two factors are most important to characterize a bond's risk: term to maturity, and credit quality of the issuer. The past few sections in this book have been discussing the implications of short-term or long-term bonds—and the premium you can earn by taking on term risk.

While maturity dates for individual bonds are explicit, funds are generally divided into three broad groups based on average maturity:

- Short-term (1 to 5 years)

- Intermediate-term (5 to 10 years)

- Long-term (more than 10 years)

As you'd expect, you can also earn a premium by taking on additional risks. The biggest of these would be investing in bonds with lower credit quality, which have increased risk of default. But other premiums can be earned for bonds that can be "called" or paid back early—depriving investors anticipated return when interest rates drop. Next we will look at credit ratings and why we normally want only the highest quality.

Credit Quality or Default Risk

KEY CONCEPTS:

- Credit quality ratings are measured on a scale that generally ranges from AAA (highest) to D (lowest).

- Treasuries are low cost, don't require diversification, and are the highest credit quality.

- Even the highest quality corporate bonds should be purchased in mutual funds because they lack price transparency and require diversification.

- High-yield corporate bonds should be avoided because they are more correlated with the stock market, illiquid, and have additional reasons for being called early.

Credit quality indicates the market's assessment on whether a bond is likely to be repaid on schedule.

This is determined by several major rating firms. Here is how Standard & Poor ratings map onto a simple style guide.[31]

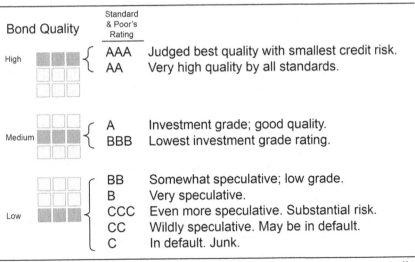

Bond Quality		Standard & Poor's Rating	
High		AAA	Judged best quality with smallest credit risk.
		AA	Very high quality by all standards.
Medium		A	Investment grade; good quality.
		BBB	Lowest investment grade rating.
Low		BB	Somewhat speculative; low grade.
		B	Very speculative.
		CCC	Even more speculative. Substantial risk.
		CC	Wildly speculative. May be in default.
		C	In default. Junk.

We recommend U.S. Treasuries and low-cost bond funds that are assigned to an overall rating of high to very-high quality..

The rating agencies each use slightly different nomenclature and fund companies have minor variations of the 9 box style guide, but the concept is the same.

Who should you loan your money to?

Many wise investors approach this like they approach their stock investments and simply invest in the total bond market by using a low-cost index fund. Since this is weighted to match the overall bond market, most of the funds will be U.S. Treasuries. This approach is extremely diversified and highly recommended. If you are not choosing a Treasuries fund, or a total bond market fund, then you need to look a little closer about what you are investing in.

You are choosing who you will loan your money to—or more precisely, who will issue the bond. Some people call simple bonds, like U.S. Treasuries, *plain vanilla bonds*, because they don't have special ingredients—like a "call provision". Homeowners are actually familiar with this concept if they use a mortgage to purchase their house. In this case, the banks are loaning money at specified rate while the homeowners want a *call provision* to be able to refinance their mortgage if interest rates become significantly lower.

I will discuss the important types of bonds in this section.

U.S. Treasuries

Prices for Treasuries are highly transparent and the market is highly liquid. Many mutual fund providers like Vanguard or Fidelity waive the transaction costs for new issues bought at auction, making these commodities with low to zero transaction costs. Investors may also purchase them directly from TreasuryDirect.gov. The bonds are as straightforward as I have described with no complicated call provisions. Interest is subject to federal income tax, but exempt from state or local income taxes.

U.S. Treasury Bills, Notes, and Bonds are the standards by which other bonds are measured because we essentially ascribe their likelihood of default to be zero.

Treasury instruments with a maturity of up to six months are called Treasury *bills*. Treasury bills are issued at a price less their face value (or, "discounted") and the interest is paid in the form of the price rising toward that face value (or, "par") at maturity. Treasury instruments with a maturity of two to ten years are called *notes*; and maturities beyond ten years are called *bonds*.[32]

Sidebar: Buying Treasuries at Auction is Easy

One option is TreasuryDirect.gov where you can buy and redeem securities directly from the U.S. Department of the Treasury in paperless electronic form.

At Fidelity, Schwab, and E-TRADE, you can buy Treasuries online for no commission. Vanguard also waives their fee for online auction orders if your account is above $100,000. Other brokers charge commissions. TD Ameritrade, for instance, charges $25.

A secondary market exists for the time between a new issue and the bond maturity. Everyone charges a fee to buy/sell Treasuries on the secondary market because they have to match sellers up with buyers.

Treasury Inflation Protected Securities (TIPS) are special U.S. Treasury Bonds where the face value changes with the Consumer Price Index (CPI) and is paid at maturity. The coupon rate is lower than a nominal Treasury bond with the same maturity but both the principal and the interest payments are indexed to inflation. TIPS are a good hedge against *unexpected* inflation.

Series I Savings Bonds (I Bonds) are government savings bonds issued by the U.S. Treasury that offer inflation protection. I Bonds offer tax-deferral for up to 30 years and are free from state and local taxation. I Bonds are not marketable securities and cannot be traded in the secondary market.

These are currently limited to $10,000 per year per social security number so I will not expand upon these here but suffice it to say that, like bank-issued CDs, these are slightly cumbersome to set-up but can be more attractive than Treasuries for individual investors and excellent short summaries can be found here:

www.Bogleheads.org/wiki/I_bonds

www.Bogleheads.org/wiki/I_Bonds_vs_TIPS

Agency Bonds

U.S. Government Agency Bonds include mortgage-backed securities or other asset-backed securities backed by the government, and by government-sponsored enterprises, such as Fannie Mae and Freddie Mac, that are not explicitly backed by the U.S. government.

Government-sponsored enterprises issue bonds to support their mandates, which typically involve ensuring certain segments of the population—like farmers, students and homeowners—are able to borrow at affordable rates. Examples include Fannie Mae, Freddie Mac, and the Tennessee Valley Authority. Yields are higher than government bonds, representing their higher level of risk, though are still considered to be on the lower end of the risk spectrum. Some income from agency bonds, like Fannie Mae and Freddie Mac are taxable. Others are exempt from state and local taxes.[33]

Agency bonds include the world of **mortgage-backed securities**. Banks and other lending institutions pool mortgages and submit them to quasi-government agencies which turn them into securities that investors can buy that are backed by income from people repaying their mortgages. This raises money so the lenders can offer more mortgages. Examples of MBS issuers include Fannie Mae, and Freddie Mac, which are public companies, but their obligations do not carry the full faith and credit of the U.S. government. Mortgage-backed bonds have a yield that typically exceeds high-grade corporate bonds. The major risk of these bonds is if borrowers repay their mortgages in a "refinancing boom" it could shorten the investment's average life and lower its yield. These bonds are also risky if many people default on their mortgages.

One of my mantras is "don't invest in things I don't understand" and mortgage-backed-securities fall in this category of very complicated financial instruments—despite their stellar credit rating. It sure seemed like this category surprised a lot of people in the sub-prime mortgage crisis of 2007.

John C. Bogle also recommends the Vanguard Intermediate-Term Bond Index Fund.[34] It is very similar to the Total Bond Market Index Fund except does not include the "bond-like" mortgage-backed securities. It includes both more Treasuries and more investment-grade corporate bonds.

International bond funds invest in a range of taxable bonds issued by foreign governments and corporations. The argument against investing in these is that they don't offer anything beyond the rich choices that already exist in the U.S. bond markets. Worse, investors are not compensated for the currency rate risks which are introduced. The argument in favor of these is that they help investors diversify by spreading interest rate and economic risk across the globe. I'm not an expert about this, but I am not even tempted.

Corporate Bonds

Investment-grade corporate bonds range from high-grade down to medium-grade producing slightly higher expected yields. Only funds should be considered at, or below, this level to ensure diversification, low-cost, and liquidity.

High-yield bond funds include bonds rated below investment-grade. They sometimes also called high income, high opportunity, or aggressive income bond funds. They are regarded to be high-credit risks and because of their default risk they are generally called "junk" bonds. Proponents of actively managed funds (not me!), and speculators of all sorts, are going to be tempted to look at these.

Special Types of Bonds

Municipal bond funds. States, cities, counties and towns issue bonds to pay for public projects (roads, sewers) and finance other activities. The majority of munis are exempt from federal income taxes and, in most cases, also exempt from state and local taxes if the investor is a resident in the state of issuance. As a result, the yields tend to be lower, but still may provide more after-tax income for investors in higher tax brackets.[35]

Even though bonds seem to come in flavors ranging from vanilla to whiskey hazelnut—they are all just ice-cream. And most of the time vanilla works just fine. Boring—maybe.

We've covered the bonds I think you need to know about, but there are others. Flavors are really unlimited.

Stick With High Quality

In the prior chapter we looked at bond maturity and term risk (interest rate risk). This chapter we have looked at credit quality and the risk of default from the issuer (the entity we loan our money to). Credit quality (or, risk of default) is the second of the two important factors that characterize bonds. While buying Individual Treasury Notes and CDs is often smart and attractive, buying lower quality bonds is usually not if your total bond investments is less than $500,000—because of cost and liquidity. Low-cost mutual funds offer an attractive alternative. We can summarize this as three levels of increasing risk:

- Low Risk: Bond or fund's average rating: AAA or AA.

- Medium: Average rating below AA, but BBB or better.

- Higher Risk: Average credit rating is below BBB.

Staying with the highest quality bonds (AAA and AA) is desirable because they are the least correlated with the stock market. Some experts suggest staying away from lower quality bonds because they tend to correlate with the stock market at the worst times. It's better to take risks in the stock market and use bonds to anchor the portfolio.

Municipal bonds have their own ratings and typically range from very low for infrastructure projects (e.g., water and sewer plants) to occasionally higher risks for projects like new hospitals.

This brings us, finally, to the central point of this book and your most important investment decision: What is the right allocation of stocks and bonds for *you*?

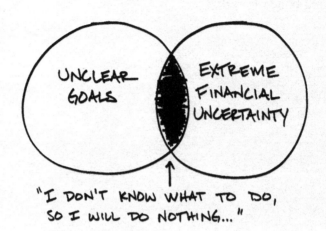

Sketch by Carl Richards at BehaviorGap.com

Build The Bond Portion Of Your Portfolio

Bonds are simple and essential in every portfolio. This part of the book is about you.

- What is your portfolio?
- How much of that should be in bonds?
- Which bonds should you choose?

A "portfolio" is an overly fancy word—but it will do. We need a way of thinking about what we have, and typically it is spread around in different forms (house, car, stocks), in a variety of accounts (banks, investments, retirement plans, Social Security expectations), and people (spouses, partners). The concept of a portfolio gives us a way to make good decisions and then get on with our lives.

Of all the decisions you'll make, the allocation between stocks and bonds is the most important.

It is tempting to think that deciding which fund to own will determine your success, but it is very minor compared to your big decisions.

Start by asking yourself: *What are you investing for?*

Start With Your Goals.

KEY CONCEPTS:

- Plans only work if you make them

- A one-page plan will do

- Strive for a first draft now; improve it later

- Focus on high-priority goals

If you watch my video tutorials you know that I think everyone should have a 1-page plan that indicates some goals and how much money you will need for them. Write down your objectives and priorities. Don't worry about correctness. Just strive for a *first draft*. You can improve it over time.

Key point: The best return on your time (ever) will be the time you spend setting goals.

Does it need to be written? I think so. But written on a napkin would be fine if you'll promise to look at it at least once a year. Can you remember it instead? No. Write it down. One of your decisions needs to be your ratio of stocks/bonds investments and you'll be very tempted to change them (in a bad way) every year if it is not in writing.

Start with a list and use placeholder estimates until you can improve them. For example:

Goal	$Needed	When
Retirement	$1,000,000	Beginning in 20+ years
House Renovation	$ 60,000	Hire in 1 year
Newer Car	$ 20,000	Buy in 1 year
Child's College Ed	$ 200,000	Needed in 6-10 years

Create a realistic plan to finance at least *all* your high-priority goals.

Key point: Retirement is so costly it should be a primary focus for everybody.

There are significant advantages to begin saving for retirement as early as possible. It's understandable that you may want to secure your short-term goals first, but you should consider resisting this temptation and maximize available tax-advantaged retirement savings options first. Find a balance of both. Only *you* can decide!

As a benefit to employees, many employers offer to match a portion of your retirement contributions. This match is like giving yourself a raise and may add a significant sum to your savings.

If you have high-interest loans and high-interest credit card balances, they must be a high priority. These are insidious and often lead to fees. Make it a priority to drive fees from your life! Wave warning flags at yourself if you own investments earning less than your auto loan or credit card interest—this is using debt to finance your investments and this magnifies your level of risk.

Saving to fund children's college education may be an example of a high want. If your budget includes saving for this, you should consider the tax-advantaged vehicles that are available.

Short-term needs that are coming up in the next five years must be separated out for targeted short-term investments. There isn't enough time to risk this in the stock market.

For example, Ruth is 35 years old and is on track for saving for the goals listed above. Money for her short-term goals is invested in short-term bonds. Her college savings is invested in a fund that is 60% stocks / 40% bonds which she will gradually change to a 100% bond allocation over the next six years. And her retirement is allocated 75% stock / 25% bonds which she plans to shift towards bonds at 1% per year.

Estimate what you will need for retirement (see sidebar). This is usually the biggest line item and necessary to establish a plan and view your investment portfolio in proper context. Really, anything less is just wishful thinking. Take a minute to think about this.

After you've taken a stab at *your* financial needs, you'll want to compare this with *your* current situation, *your* net worth. The gap between where you are, what you will need, and your timeframe govern how much investment risk you *need* to take if your goals are to be met.

Usually people are not saving and investing enough to achieve their goals. Then it's back to the drawing board: you will either need to work longer (retiring later is not always possible), save more, or lower your retirement goals. Once you have a first draft plan that supports your goals, you're off and running! Review and revise it every year, and you'll discover that it gradually improves with time.

And, only if the ability and willingness are truly there, you could consider a high exposure to stocks, according to your unique circumstances—your investment objectives, your time horizon, your level of comfort with risk, and your financial resources.

Sometimes a young person is able to handle considerable risk, maybe towards 90% stocks, and rely on time to iron out volatile short-term returns. They are on a solid career path, save religiously from every paycheck, and have an established emergency fund in case of inevitable surprises.

Similarly, some seniors have adequate retirement income from Social Security or a pension and can continue to let stocks dominate their investments.

Saving for retirement is almost always your biggest goal. Next is a simple way to include a number in your goals. Yes, choose a specific number for a goal—you can always change it. But writing a number down is one step closer to creating a plan that works.

Is it difficult to estimate your retirement expenses? Then use a placeholder number—you can improve this estimate later. Are you seeing a pattern here? Any plan is better than no plan. And if you promise to look at it every year for at least 1 hour—it will become a pretty good plan!

Sidebar: Estimate What You'll Need For Retirement

First imagine being retired and what your income would need to be to support it. If you are young, it might be worth asking your parents to get a reference to calibrate your own plan. If you are 40-60, it is generally less than your current income because you will no longer contribute to retirement accounts, your children will be on their own, and hopefully your mortgage and other loans will be paid by then.

For example, here a single investor estimates his retirement living expenses will be $60,000 per year and that he expects $20,000 per year from Social Security beginning at this Full Retirement Age (age 65 to 67, depending on year of birth). In order to fund this gap, he will need to save one million dollars. The inputs to this rule-of-thumb are all in today's dollars to cover inflation-adjusted expenses for 30 years (ages 65 until 95).

Estimated Need	$	60,000	per year
less expect from Social Security at age 65	$	20,000	per year
less expect from any pensions	$	-	
less expected from any annuities you own	$	-	
Estimated Need to Fund from Investments	$	40,000	per year

Approximate Investment Portfolio that would accomplish that (still using today's dollars): 25 x $40,000 = $1,000,000.

Note: multiplying by 25 is the same as the Trinity study rule-of-thumb that a 4% draw from your investments can usually cover inflation-adjusted expenses for 30 years. Much more sophisticated models don't add more certainty.

Do you want to be conservative? A more cautious approach would presume that Social Security will be reduced by 20% (making the gap you need to fund larger) and that the market might have lower returns (making the multiplier larger). You won't find a crystal ball, but do the best you can and you can be in the ballpark.

Sidebar: Pensions, Social Security, and Annuities are not bonds.

They <u>do</u> reduce the amount you need to fund your retirement from your investment portfolio, but they <u>do not</u> count as bonds as you consider bonds allocation and your stocks/bonds ratio for your associated level of investment risk. Consider this: Dr. Clever has an identical situation to the prior sidebar example and has determined 50/50 is the correct allocation between stocks and bonds, so he should invest it $500K in stocks and $500K in bonds. But he wants to view his Social Security as an equivalent lump sum.

To fund $60,000 per year he figures he needs a portfolio of 25 x $60,000 = $1.5 million, of which $750K should be in bonds and $750K should be in stocks. Next he decides his Social Security is equivalent to owning a 25 x $20,000 = $500,000 bond. So, turning to his investment portfolio he needs $250K bonds and $750K in stocks.

Can you see that this 75/25 allocation is dramatically riskier than the 50/50 allocation—his desired level of risk? Consider the impact of a stock market crash while he is largely living off his invested savings. He has much more exposed to the stock market and this is clearly riskier.

Similarly, if we were to consider pensions or annuities as a bond-like lump sum, then the effect would be to shift our actual investment portfolio towards stocks, potentially making it much riskier than intended. Our goal is to be fully aware of how much risk we are taking, and try not to take more risk than is necessary.

Homeowners wonder about whether to treat the value of their home as an investment. Start with my short answer, then adjust it for your circumstances. It is both best and easiest to retire debt-free with your mortgage paid. If the interest on your debt is higher than the interest you are earning on your bonds, then the reason is obvious. Some people like to consider debt like negative bonds—then your investment risk is honestly revealed.

Many retire debt-free and don't count their house value as an investment—but rather a provision for future rent payments as their needs change. But those that don't have large savings locked up in their house as an investment do need to include a monthly housing cost when coming up with their living expenses.

Each of us, individually, must determine how much risk to take and how that translates to stocks and bonds.

How Much Risk Is Right For You?

KEY CONCEPTS:

- Understand how much risk you are taking.

- Assess your risk profile and learn the corresponding ratio of stocks/bonds.

- "Own your age in bonds," or any other plan, might be fine. It is only a good plan if you can stick to it.

The Financial Industry Regulatory Authority (FINRA) warns that: "The single biggest mistake bond investors make is reaching for yield after interest rates have declined. Don't be tempted by higher yields offered by bonds with lower credit qualities, or be focused only on gains that resulted during the prior period. Yield is one of many factors an investor should consider when buying a bond. And never forget: With higher yield comes higher risk."[36]

Taking risk isn't inherently a bad thing. But it's bad to not understand and control how much risk you're taking.

What's An Investment Portfolio?

Your investment portfolio is simply the sum of all the taxable savings and investment accounts and all tax-advantaged investment accounts for *both* you and your spouse. Always consider this as a whole because money is interchangeable—it doesn't matter what account pays when you use it, but it does matter what you hold in these different types of accounts to minimize your tax costs.

Key Point: Treat your entire portfolio as a whole (include spouse). Here's what is useful to consider in your long-term portfolio:

- *Your* taxable savings/investments

- Your *spouse's* taxable savings/investments

- *Your* tax-advantaged investments (e.g., IRA, 401(k), 403(b), SEP IRA, Roth IRA, etc.)

- Your *spouse's* tax-advantaged investments

- Other valuable assets that you would not hesitate to liquidate to finance your goals (e.g., vacation time share)

- Emergency fund (3 to 6 months living expenses). This one may surprise you. But since this is the money you should save first, this will give you an immediate sense of progress. Further, you're not planning to have an emergency, right? It's there if you need it.

Then list your liabilities:

- All significant debt (beyond home mortgage), including school loans, car loans, and residual credit card debt). This may also surprise you. Some find it constructive to view this debt as "negative bonds" to determine their net asset allocation. It also helps shine a light on debt service that exceeds what your bonds are yielding.

Here is stuff you should not consider part of your investment portfolio:

- Valuable art and jewelry that you don't intend to sell.

- Cars and home furnishings that you don't intend to sell.

- Home equity (realistic market value less mortgage). You will always need a home, or will need these savings to pay rent or other senior housing.

- Savings earmarked for short-term needs (e.g., college educations, car, trips, furniture, etc.).

- Your anticipated Social Security benefit.

- Your anticipated pension and annuity benefits.

For these planning purposes, we want to focus on the saving and investment decisions that you have control over to achieve your goals.

Understand How Much Risk You're Taking

The primary factor is your allocation to the stock market. Our rule of thumb is to expect losses in the stock market up to 50% in any year. Expect this to occur multiple times during your investment lifetime. The most recent example was the stock market falling in 2008. Did you own stocks? Did you "stay the course"? Did you panic?

If you were investing during that global financial crisis, and you rebalanced to maintain your chosen stock/bond allocation throughout, then your actual behavior is a solid indicator of your risk tolerance. If you weren't, then you are untested and might easily overestimate your risk tolerance. Proceed with caution.

To assess your risk profile you must consider your ability, willingness, and need to take investment risk.

Ability to take Risk. What would be the consequences of, say, losing half of your investment wealth in the stock market later this year? Could you recover? Clearly, a high-income doctor in his/her thirties has a lot of time and opportunity to recover from a stock market crash, or several. We refer to this as *human capital* and job security, or some measure of your expected lifetime earnings. A tenured professor would also have a lot more ability to carry investment risk than, say, an auto mechanic.

But notice that the spouse of that doctor or professor may not carry that same ability, should they need to. Their income earning potentials might be poor. For this book, we will consider lifelong singles or couples and always consider all assets *combined*— because the money doesn't care which account it came from. But *you* definitely do because you can minimize or defer your income taxes.

Willingness to take risk. This is very personal. If you simply cannot stomach the risk of one (or several) serious stock market crashes during your investment timeframe then this becomes the driver.

Also remember that bond values can be volatile. Interest rate sensitivity increases with maturity—especially for long-term TIPS.[37]

The whole reason for this introspection is to avoid judging yourself as having more ability or willingness to take stock market risk than you actually have, and then do a panic sell to get out of a plunging stock market. This common investor behavior guarantees poor results!

Need to take risk. Simply saving regularly into your bank account isn't going to help most people achieve their dreams. You must take *some* investment risk. This is alleviated by starting early and using the miracle of compound interest. But for the 50-year old who is just starting to wonder about retirement, the need to start saving might be a huge wake-up call. In an earlier section we looked at the investment return you would need to get from where you are to where you want to go. But caution, there are no guarantees that by choosing higher risk you'll achieve a higher return.

One of my wise friends calls this *need to take risk* a sham in this context—that it really just indicates a need to *save* more aggressively. The implication being that it is the reckless individual that failed to save and invest, neither early, often, nor sufficiently, and hence would *need* to take more risk to achieve his/her financial goals.

Example: Building on the previous example, suppose your list concludes that your total needed for goals is $800,000. You are saving a total of 15% of your income through automatic payroll deposits into a balanced fund (60%stocks/40% bonds) and you see that a 3% real return will only grow to $600,000 by retirement. Does that mean you *need* to take more investment risk? Careful. Neither buying lottery tickets nor speculative stock investing are going to increase the likelihood of success. In this case, your decision should be governed by your ability and willingness. If you are sure you would stick with a wild ride then you could consider even higher expected risks and rewards by adding a small portion of a small-company index fund or of a small-value index fund. The other options for getting to a high goal are to earn more, save more, retire later, or reprioritize your goals.

Most of us *need* to use the miracle of compound interest to grow the market returns faster than inflation to meet our biggest goals. And once you accomplish that, you can become more conservative for that investment goal and remain more aggressive for others. For example, you might choose to leave excess wealth intended for a charity invested in the stock market.

Take Your Risk In The Stock Market, Not Bond Market

We've already discussed how interest rate risk can be controlled by choosing bonds with appropriate duration. That still means there will be short-term fluctuations, but we've also highlighted that Treasury bond fluctuations are poorly correlated with stocks (when viewed broadly over long time periods).

In his book *Common Sense on Mutual Funds,* John Bogle cites an article[38] by Laurence Siegel to tell us that, for long-term investors, risk is not short-term volatility:

"Risk is not short-term volatility, for the long-term investor can afford to ignore that. Rather, because there is no predestined rate of return, only an expected one that may not be realized, *the risk is the possibility that, in the long run, stock returns will be terrible.*"

And while John Bogle says these comments provide a healthy

reminder of the uncertainty of future returns in the financial markets, they hardly invalidate his central message: "Focusing on the long term is far superior to focusing on the short term. It is a lesson too few investors have learned."

"Remember," Bogle says, "the goal of the long-term investor is not to preserve capital in the short run, but to earn real, inflation-adjusted, long-term returns." He advises using bonds as a source of regular income and as a moderating influence on a stock portfolio, not as an alternative to stocks.[39]

Bond expert Larry Swedroe constantly makes the point that it is better to take your risk in the stock market. He looks at risk factors that investors can choose, how much they have historically been compensated for them, and concludes: "While investors have been well rewarded for taking the risks of investing in stocks in general, and specifically small stocks and value stocks, as well as for taking term risk [in bonds], they have received almost no reward for accepting corporate credit risks [in bonds].[40]

Owning long-term corporate bonds—and especially owning junk bonds—makes your portfolio more correlated with the stock market. So, a 60/40 portfolio using high-yield bonds might have the same volatility (risk) as a 70/30 portfolio using Treasury bonds—but the expected return is lower.[41]

Finally, bear in mind that investing isn't science. Returns, correlations, and standard deviations vary over different time periods. So while this is useful to help motivate common sense principles of a diversified and low-cost portfolio, don't get bogged down in this or other investing models. Keep it simple.

While saving early and often is your most important investment *habit*, the ratio of stocks to bonds is your most important investment *decision*. Choose a balance of stocks and bonds according to your unique circumstances—your investment objectives, your time horizon, your level of comfort with risk, and your financial resources.[42] Then, stick to your plan!

How Much in Bonds? How Much in Stocks?

We described how to match the duration of fixed-income investments to short-term needs—so we can set those aside for now. That money is earmarked—already spent. The rest of this book will consider our long-term investment portfolio.

It's fairly common to see asset allocations with descriptive labels—like Conservative, Moderate, Growth, or Aggressive Growth in the following picture.[43] I urge you to *not* consider these labels, but rather assess your risk tolerance more overtly. The issue is: how will you behave when there is a sudden drop in your portfolio value and it looks like it will fall further. Will you sell to get out? Or will you sell some bond funds to buy more of the falling stock funds?

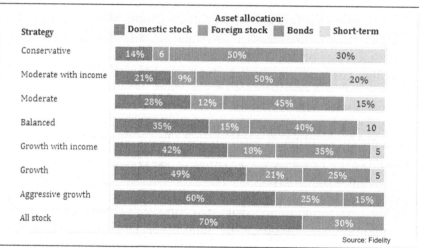

Attempting to attach English descriptions to common allocations of stocks/bonds/cash seems helpful but inadequately shows how these generally need to change with time.

It's too tempting for investors to decide their stock/bond allocation based on these labels. You're apt to *feel* attracted to a *growth* or *aggressive-growth* portfolio when the news and economy is generally positive, and then decide you want to be *moderate* or *conservative* after a spate of bad news. This is letting your emotions interfere with your plan and would be terrible, as Carl Richards brilliantly depicts in this sketch.

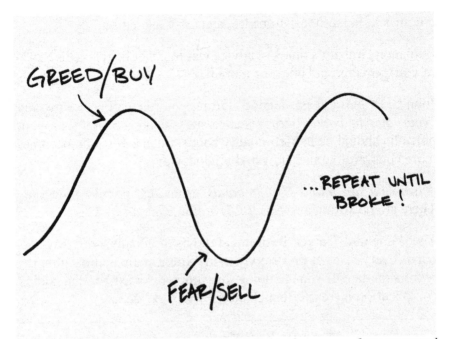

This brilliant sketch by Carl Richards illustrates how humans are forever tempted by speculation, and confusing this with investing.

The simple ratio of stocks/bonds determines the risk of your portfolio. Do you know what your ratio is? What you want it to be? Yes, it is *that* important!

Know Your Enemies:

- Inflation

- Your investing behavior—if not disciplined.

Which is Enemy #1 for you? What will you do about it? Choose your ratio of stocks/bonds; then stick to it through thick and thin.

Your Needs Change Over Time

Haven't figured out what ratio of stocks/bonds is appropriate for you yet? Don't worry—but don't put this off either. Here is some guidance to help. Happily, this isn't an area that requires precision. Rough numbers like 80/20, 70/30, or 60/40 are good enough. Author Rick Ferri cleverly observed that "being <u>close</u> is good enough when it comes to horseshoes, grenades, and asset allocation."[44]

Benjamin Graham's timeless advice was to never hold less than 25% of your portfolio in bonds, or more than 75%.[45]

John C. Bogle suggests a good starting point is to consider owning *"your age in bonds"*; for instance, if you are 45, 45% of your portfolio should be in high-quality bonds. Such a portfolio becomes more conservative in a slow and gradual way.

"Own your age minus 10% in bonds" is another popular guideline. There are no wrong answers *if it is a plan you can stick to.*

The Vanguard Target Retirement funds gradually shift towards bonds every year, at first slowly then more rapidly approaching the retirement date. If you are doing this yourself remember that adding complication increases that chance it won't get done.

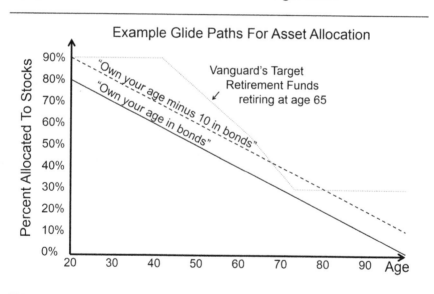

Here are some common strategies that gradually become conservative with time. What you choose is less important than sticking to it.

Before retirement, this asset allocation plan helps you decide where to deposit your new savings. In retirement, it helps you determine where to take your withdrawals from.

This ratio is the foundation of this book. This is your rock. This book is all about managing the bond portion of this rock. More important than the actual ratio is having the discipline to stick to it. Many don't, and inadvertently chase performance or sell in a panic—both with catastrophic results.

Happily, our most important investment decision costs nothing but a little time.

The loser's game is to be dazzled by the excitement and the chance to win big by hiring the right fund manager, actively trading stocks, and choosing the next winning mutual fund. This is evident from the devoted television channels, newspapers, and newsletters—and distracts us from the important decisions, and sticking to them.

John C. Bogle recognizes this behavior as "speculating" as opposed to investing—which is to own a piece of businesses that create value and are the source of all returns. He begrudges the industry that focuses on financial transactions and all the new financial products and marketing that accelerate those transactions which ultimately only subtract from value flowing to investors.[46]

Earlier in this book we talked about the two characteristics of bonds: term to maturity and credit quality. But for ordinary investors we must add a third: costs.

Three Factors For Choosing Bonds or Bond Funds:

1. Time-to-maturity
2. Credit quality of issuer
3. Costs

Sidebar: Wrong balance? What are you waiting for?

Worried about moving your correct allocation into bonds because interest rates are so low?

Instead, you're in stocks? Do you realize that stocks can lose in one day what bonds might lose in a year?

Or, do you hold cash in an attempt to avoid all risk? Well, you haven't. Bank accounts and money market funds nearly always earn less than inflation, and it is even worse after you adjust for inflation. It would be much more prudent to tip-toe back into a very conservative allocation. Get started today, even if you take monthly, or quarterly, steps toward your correct stock/bond allocation. Even baby steps will eventually get you there.

The Importance of Low Cost

KEY CONCEPTS:

- Diversifying U.S. Treasury bonds isn't as important as diversifying stocks.

- Low cost is the third important factor that determines success for bond investments: (1) time to maturity, (2) issuer credit quality, and (3) expenses and fees.

- Do-It-Yourselfers spend less.

"In Investing, You Get What You Don't Pay For." [47]

Five years ago, Samantha inherited $60,000 worth of high-tech stocks. She had an additional $40,000 in a savings account. She hired a financial advisor who replaced the stock with a mutual fund, put her savings in a bond fund, promised to keep her at this stock/bond ratio, and assured her that she will earn higher returns with their firm which will more than offset their fee which is 1% of her portfolio balance every year. The two funds have annual fees which were 0.4% and 0.3% which seemed small and she promptly forgot about.

That's pretty typical. Many financial advisors charge fees of 1% (or more) of your portfolio balance each year to provide portfolio management services as well as ongoing financial planning advice. The question to consider is whether these services are needed and whether this is a fair way to pay for these services. It's often less expensive to break the services out and pay for them separately.

To illustrate the cost of this service to Samantha, consider how her portfolio might grow with and without the all-inclusive professional services. We'll assume stocks return 7% and bonds return 3% (both below historic averages). Her investment period is from age 30 to 70, and the firm keeps her balanced at 60% stocks and 40% bonds. The total value would be $491,000 after 40 years.

In contrast, she could set up an account at one of the mutual fund giants, choose an excellent balanced fund (60% / 40%) with an annual fee of 0.16%, and have an end value of $771,000. The difference of $280,000 went to her financial advisor's firm!

That's right! Now, there will be no way to make Samantha feel good when she learns this. Samantha takes all the risk, and her advisor would now own more than one-third of that total in exchange for their services. The question she really needs to ask herself is, "Did I get good value for what I paid this advisor?" For some the answer might be yes. But for many, I think this eye-opening reality is enough to help them understand that they can learn to *take control of their finances* and that this is one of the keys to achieving financial independence.

If you suspect that this book has a strong bias towards managing your own investments, you would be right! I think most people are smart enough and just need to be shown how, step-by-step. Yes, if Samantha (or you!) has something complicated that she needs advice on she should be happy to pay a fair price for that. But make that a separate and reasonable fee for that specific service.

How Much To Diversify Bonds?

Diversifying the highest quality bonds has neither the same importance nor benefits as diversifying stocks. The two main parameters you would consider diversifying are the *credit quality* of the issuer and the *term* of the bond.

With Treasury bonds, the most liquid investment in the world, trading costs are extremely low. And since there is no credit risk, you don't need to use a mutual fund to diversify credit quality. Instead, you can buy individual Treasuries on your own, saving the expense ratio of a mutual fund. Or buy government insured CDs from a bank or credit union for the similar benefits. Smaller investments? Keep it simple. Just use a low-cost mutual fund, and get on with life!

Diversification of lower quality bonds would be important. But remember: The single biggest mistake bond investors make is reaching for yield after interest rates have declined. Don't be tempted by high-yield bonds.

Is it important to diversify the term of the bonds? Not really. It is important to match the bond type and duration with the investment goal as we discussed earlier. You can accomplish this yourself with individual bonds or CDs, by a simple bond ladder, or with a constant duration bond fund.

Don't try to time the market. Buy what you need now. As hard as it is to time the stock market, it's even harder to time the bond market. Avoid speculating on interest rates. Decisions are too often made on where rates have been rather than where they are going. Instead, stick to the investment strategy that will best help you achieve your goals and objectives.[48]

Earlier we discussed the pros and cons of international bonds, but they seem to cancel each other. So when in doubt, choose simplicity. *Stick with U.S. bonds.* John C. Bogle emphatically agrees, saying multiple times over his career: "When there are multiple solutions, choose the simplest one."[49]

The Importance of Low Cost

Low cost remains essential to success—basically, you get to keep what you don't give away. "So if we pay nothing, we get everything."[50] That's our goal—to keep what our investments earn.

Unlike stocks, where your return is tied to a company's degree of success, the interest you receive for a bond (loaning your money) is largely uncoupled from that success. There is little value the manager for a fund of high-quality bonds can add—other than to attempt market timing.

It is hard for investors to keep costs (expense ratio) for bond funds less than stock funds, but the expected returns are certainly less so these costs take a bigger chunk. If your bond fund yields 2.5% right now, just 1% in fees or expenses cuts your return by 40%.

Consequently, owning individual federally-insured CDs or Treasuries can be a useful strategy. Very few CDs or individual Treasury bonds may be sufficient on your bond side, whereas owning so few individual stocks would be folly. It would for speculating, but not for investing.

General Guidance For Selecting Bonds

- Use bond funds (or a recurring ladder) for future needs that don't have a calendar date. This will generally become most of your bond investments.

- Use individual bonds or non-recurring ladders for specific obligations. Generally prefer CDs, and US Treasuries to keep costs down. Diversification helps very little here.

- Check a fund's *duration*. Keep the *duration* shorter than when you will need this money.

- Stick to short- or intermediate-term for the best risk/reward. An exception might be longer-term TIPS.[51].

- Stick to the highest quality bond funds or individual bonds rated AAA or AA. Don't chase performance. Risk is better rewarded in the stock market.

- Split your bond investments between TIPS and nominal bonds to hedge for unexpected inflation.

- Deferring taxes is very valuable. Bonds are "inefficient" in that they get taxed at a higher rate than stock investments. Hold taxable bonds in tax-advantaged accounts like IRAs and 401(k) accounts, at least when interest payments are significant.

- Use index funds for liquidity, low cost and diversification.

- Staying with U.S.-only is fine.

- Be wary about buying individual bonds because of cost and liquidity. An exception is buying new issues of U.S. Treasuries, both nominal bonds and TIPS.

- Plan to reinvest your interest earned. This allows the power of compounding to work on your behalf.

- Don't try to time the market.

Five Low-Cost Strategies You Can Do Yourself

#1 Low-Cost Mutual Funds: The easiest winning strategy for simple long-term investing in intermediate-term highest quality bonds is a low-cost bond index mutual fund. The annual cost (ER) for both these is only 0.10% for investments over $10,000.

FIBIX Fidelity Spartan Intermediate Treasuries Fund (cost = 0.20%)

VFITX Vanguard Intermediate Treasuries Mutual fund (cost 0.20%)

#2 Low-Cost ETFs: If your transactions are long-term and infrequent, then you can consider an ETF fund if you don't have good low-cost mutual fund choices. For examples:

AGG iShares Total Bond Market Index Fund ETF (cost = 0.08%)

BND Vanguard Total Bond Market Index Fund ETF (cost = 0.08%)

#3 Opportunistic CDs and I bonds: Earlier we showed that if you are willing to put in the time and effort, you can actively mine long-term CDs with above-market yields and attractive withdrawal penalties. Also true for Inflation Savings Bonds (I Bonds).

#4 Opportunistic TIPS: The yield for TIPS varies between roughly -1% and +3%, so one strategy for those who insist on watching the market is to convert the bond holdings to TIPS when their real yield exceeds, say, 2%. Is this market timing (which is bad)? You decide. To me it is not speculating on the future, but rather locking in attractive rates the same way homeowners do when mortgage interest rates fall very low.

#5 Individual Bonds for Lowest Cost

Building your own fund only makes sense to me if you are using Treasuries and your goal is lowest possible costs. For some perspective, consider owning $100,000 in Fidelity Spartan Intermediate Term Treasury Fund. The expense ratio for this is currently 0.1%, which means you pay only $100 per year. I think that's a bargain for most people! But suppose the bond portion of your portfolio is bigger, or your expense ratio (operating cost) is higher? I, for one, have a hard time paying hundreds or thousands of dollars each and every year for something I can easily learn to buy and own for free!

Treasuries (includes TIPS) are attractive because they can often be purchased and held without a sales commission and annual fees, and they don't need diversification because most consider U.S. Treasury bonds to be free of credit risk.

Earlier, we made the case for CDs. Some people use DepositAccounts.com to find CDs with attractive rates and are careful to observe the FDIC limits of $250,000 per account. Note that while the market where bonds can be traded is extremely efficient, there is quite a lot of variety in CD rates. This is because big institutional money cannot participate, and also because banks use these rates as a promotion to capture new customers. Until recently, I didn't own any CDs because: (1) I don't like the extra research and complexity of working with multiple institutions, and (2) they lack the liquidity of bond funds. But I certainly know people who do use this to their advantage. Just make sure you understand the penalty if you liquidate early—it's typically at least a few months of interest.

Individual corporate bonds are another animal. Their costs are expensive and not transparent and diversification becomes a necessity. Mutual funds and ETFs are definitely the preferred way to own even the highest quality corporate bonds. Institutional investors have the upper hand. There is no organized "bond market" so access is one advantage they have. They can also trade at preferred rates/prices. If you are tempted to own corporate bonds funds, you must do additional homework so that you know exactly what bonds are owned by the fund and the costs of the fund.

This chapter introduced the third of the three important factors that characterize bond investments: term, quality, and costs.

One of your biggest costs is hard to recognize because it isn't going to be listed on your account statement—but you don't need to be a genius to recognize that ordinary tax brackets will take a huge bite out of what your investments earn. You need to be a little tax savvy.

100

Taxes Matter

KEY CONCEPTS:

- Use tax-advantaged retirement accounts to your advantage.

- Start early to build a tax-advantaged account so that you'll have room to hold bonds there when you'll need it.

Taxes are complicated, and every good citizen must pay their fair share. We can say a few more things about taxes with certainty:

Tax-advantaged accounts are valuable. There are two flavors of these. The *tax-deferred* variety includes the IRA, 401(k), 403b, SEP IRA, and Simple IRA. You don't have to pay tax on money you earn this year that you invest in one of these accounts, because you will pay tax when you use it in retirement. But, that's huge. Paying your taxes way off in the future is a tremendous advantage. Inflation lets you pay those taxes with cheaper dollars, and for many, their future tax rate will be at a lower level in retirement.

Tax-free is the other variety. These are Roth IRAs and Roth 401k's. You pay tax today, but not on the earnings. These also are ideal for young adults because you can withdraw the principal contributed without a penalty if you need to, making it an emergency *Emergency-Fund*.

We can also say, with certainty, that if your investments are *all* in tax-advantaged accounts, fund placement will not make much difference to your returns. (But, put highest expected growth in your Roth accounts because they are forever tax-free.)

Finally, investors need to know that different sources of investment income are taxed at different rates in a taxable account. Regular bond interest currently gets taxed at your ordinary tax bracket rate, whereas both qualified stock distributions and capital gains from long-term stock holdings are currently taxed at a much lower rate.

Avoid Painting Yourself Into A Corner

Ken the coroner knows that stocks get preferential when owned in an ordinary taxable account. So, ever since college, he has been buying a low-cost broadly diversified stock fund. That was the good advice, right? Almost.

Now that he has retirement on his mind, and after living through the traumatic markets of 2001 and 2008, he would like to shift to bonds. In fact, he has heard that "owning your age in bonds" is a good rule of thumb, or at least a starting point to consider. He is fifty years old and he would like to sell half of his stocks to put in bonds. Uh oh. He is stuck. He can't change his stock/bond allocation without taking a huge tax hit, let's say 15% capital gains tax on a gain (value above amount invested) of say $200,000 makes a tax cost of $30,000. The coroner painted himself into a corner. Ouch. Should he pay that, or stay in the riskier 100% stocks?

His buddy, Bob the Boglehead, knows two things that the coroner didn't. First, it is valuable to let your money grow in a tax advantaged account. So, while he made the same investments as Ken every year—the same after they both paid their taxes—Bob's investments contributions were *one-third higher*. In other words, Ken is in the 25% tax bracket so he earns $6,000 in order to invest $4,500 in stocks in his taxable account and pays a $1,500 tax bill. Bob is in the same tax bracket, earns and contributes $6,000 to his traditional IRA which is a deduction on his tax return so he saves $1,500 in his tax bill.

So, while both Ken and Bob have the same amount to spend every year after taxes, Bob's IRA investments grow to be 33% bigger because he is contributing more and deferring those taxes until later. The advantage to most people is that they can access that money with a lower tax rate once they retire. A second wonderful benefit is that all transactions within the IRA don't impact his income taxes, so he can shift the allocation to bonds to control his risk at no cost. Wow. Tax-advantaged retirement accounts are valuable for everybody!

Another thing we can say with certainty. Not only are taxes complicated, they vary from year to year, from state to state, and every individual situation is different. So the last solid thing I can say is that to optimize your tax situation you must do a little scenario analysis which will involve assumptions about future market returns, future tax policy and your future personal situation.

If you choose to have a taxable account, then *normally* the conventional wisdom has been to put your stock investments there and to put your bonds in tax-advantaged account. This assumes that you will hold your stocks. Tax on capital gains is not only deferred until you sell the stocks, but the tax is at a lower rate.

This advice has become a lot weaker for the past few years because bond yields have been at record lows. To illustrate, let's take an investor in the 25% tax bracket and examine the annual tax on stocks in a taxable account:

(Qualified stock dividends) x 15% tax rate = tax cost for stocks

A total market stock index typically yields about 2% of its value as qualified stock dividends for a tax cost of 2% x 15% = 0.30% plus deferred capital gains taxes.

The annual tax for bonds in a taxable account would be:

(Bond dividends) x 25% tax rate = tax cost for bonds

When bond yields are very low (say, 1%), then the tax cost would be 1% x 25% = 0.25%, or slightly more efficient than stocks. But when bond yields are higher (say, 3%), then the tax cost would be 3% x 25% = 0.75%, which is less efficient than stocks.

One more point is worth making. It is generally true that investors need to become more conservative as they age. Growing some stock funds in a tax-advantaged account creates the space for the desired bond holding later in your career. Not only can the stocks be gradually converted to bonds without any tax consequence in that account, but annual rebalancing to maintain desired risk level can be done without creating any additional current taxes.

103

It's complicated and constantly changing. Everyone needs to engage in lifelong learning.

High-income individuals need to additionally learn about municipal bonds and where to hold them, state taxes and which bonds are exempt from these, and the advantages of tax loss harvesting in taxable accounts.

That's it! Perhaps all you need to know about bonds, although lifelong learning is a part of responsible investing. I'll try to put all the key points from this book on the next page and a half. See if you are comfortable with each of these, and if you are you will do well. *Investing doesn't require high IQ; it requires discipline.*

Summary of Key Points in This Book

Bonds are like IOUs. Buying a bond means you are lending out your money.

Bonds are also called fixed-income securities because the cash flow from them is fixed.

Stocks are equity; bonds are debt.

The key reason to purchase bonds is because stocks are risky. Bonds both stabilize and diversify your portfolio.

The issuers of bonds are governments and corporations.

Certificates of Deposit (CDs) are similar to traditional bonds and are issued by banks or credit unions.

A bond is characterized by its face value, coupon rate, maturity and issuer.

Bonds do not appreciate in price like stocks do, but their prices do fluctuate over time.

Yield is the rate of return you get on a bond.

When price goes up, yield goes down, and vice versa.

When interest rates rise, the price of bonds in the market falls, and vice versa. Nobody can predict future interest rates. Don't try.

Bills, notes and bonds are all fixed-income securities classified by maturity.

Government bonds are the safest bonds. Don't invest in bonds with less than investment-grade credit quality.

Government-insured CDs are sometimes even better than bonds.

All other bonds are not risk free. It's always possible—especially in the case of corporate bonds—for the borrower to default on the debt payments.

High-risk/high-yield bonds are known as junk bonds

You can purchase most bonds through a brokerage or bank. If you are a U.S. citizen, you can buy government bonds through TreasuryDirect.gov.

Often, brokers will not charge a commission to buy bonds but will mark-up the price instead. However, many brokers will sell U.S. Treasuries without any fees.

Bond mutual funds provide liquidity, are convenient, and many are both excellent and low cost.

The duration of a bond, or a bond fund, is a measure of its price sensitivity to interest rate changes.

Individual bonds have declining duration. This is useful.

Bond funds have constant duration. This is also useful.

Treasury Inflation Protected Securities (TIPS) are bonds issued at a lower yield but the principal is indexed to inflation.

TIPS are better than traditional bonds if future inflation is greater than current expectations.

Low cost is key.

Your allocation to bonds is your most important investing decision.

Choose a balance of stocks and bonds according to your unique circumstances—your investment objectives, your time horizon, your level of comfort with risk, and your financial resources.

Many people choose a simple way to manage this balance, like "own your age in bonds," or "own your age minus 10% in bonds." What you choose is much less important than sticking to your plan!

Inflation and our investing behavior (if not disciplined) are the two worst enemies for investors.

Start early. Keep it simple. Stick with your plan. And live life fully.

Time to check in ...

How's that "classic investor stew" coming along?

Do you better understand about how bonds work, how much to own, and what kind to buy?

That's our sole purpose for making these books and the free videos on our website—to help you and your investments weather all the financial storms that will inevitable pass through during your investing lifetime. We wish everyone to achieve common life goals such as owning a home, providing for yourself or your family, taking fun vacations, and retiring in comfort—all free from financial stress.

The favor of a review...

Has this book been helpful so far?

Reviews, ratings and comments about this guide on Amazon, or on your favorite blog, are much appreciated. If you've enjoyed the walk, you can leave a review here:
www.amazon.com/dp/0985800402

Here are three reasons you might consider for leaving a review:
- Reviews help others to find this book, and decide whether to read it.
- You help me to sell more books. *This is how we pay for the direct expenses of this not-for-profit educational project (for which I volunteer my time).*
- I get to hear what you think. *I read all the reviews of my books and love to hear what readers have to say.*

If you enjoyed this book, I would REALLY appreciate you putting up a one or two sentence review on Amazon.

Simply click where it says "xx customer reviews" next to the overall star rating, then click the button "Write a customer review." If you have a moment, I'd be grateful for your time.

Example Portfolios (both good and bad)

The following are example asset allocations (AA) to illustrate common mistakes. They use funds from Vanguard and Fidelity because I know them and they are outstanding. However, outstanding portfolios can be also built from funds from other companies such as T. Rowe Price, Dodge & Cox, Schwab, and others.

There are hundreds of variations of what a reasonable investment portfolio might look like. So use these examples as a learning tool and something to compare with your own thoughts and situations against. See whether you agree with the assessments I offer for each.

Costs matter, and annual expenses (usually called "expense ratio" or ER) are depicted after specific funds listed. Generally < 0.5% is ok, and > 1.0% is bad.

These are the examples that follow:

Simon Simple	Age 25, single, 80/20, 5-stars
Young family	Age 32, married, 70/30, 5-stars
Larry Latecomer	Age 45, single, 100% stocks, 2-stars
M.T. Nesters	Age 50, married, 60/40, 5-stars
Lonny and Lola Lowcost	Age 60, married, 50/50, 5-stars
Al and Shill Pay	Age 70, married, 80/20, 2-stars

To get your thinking started, let's assume you will need Social Security and/or Pension plus *half your final salary* to cover your retirement expenses each year. You will need invested savings to replace that half salary. The nest egg required for drawing an inflation-adjusted 4% per year for 30 years would be:

Required Assets = (FinalSalary / 2) x 25 = 12.5 x FinalSalary

Investment expert and popular blogger Mike Piper is a big advocate of simple portfolios that automatically rebalance as one more step towards keeping human temptations from inadvertently making bad portfolio decisions. He lists these as common portfolio mistakes[52]:

- Not wanting to save and invest until late in your career
- Holding a large portion of your total net worth in any one stock (especially your employer's stock!)
- Bailing out of the market *after* big crashes
- Getting involved with daily trading of individual stocks, foreign currencies, commodities, etc.
- Paying a sizable commission every time you invest, only to invest in funds that have high ongoing costs as well
- Listening to certain personal finance "experts" on the radio when they say you can safely withdraw 8% from your portfolio every year throughout retirement

See if you can spot these in the examples that follow. Think about your own portfolio.

Would you like to listen in on some real portfolios discussed by knowledgeable people that are generous with their help? Find these discussion threads by exactly typing the following into your Google search box:

```
site:bogleheads.org "current retirement assets"
```

After you have learned from others, take time to consider your own situation. The Bogleheads have some helpful tools and you will find the links in these endnotes will help you to get started. First read *Investment Planning*[53] followed by *Asking Portfolio Questions*[54].

Your financial success requires a commitment to lifelong learning—not a big commitment, just an ongoing curiosity. The Bogleheads' forum is a wonderful resource. Ask any and all questions. This forum is loaded with some pretty astute individuals with no motive other than to help others succeed financially. It's one of the gems of the internet.

Simon, age 25, single, 80/20

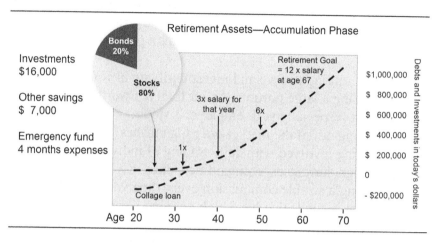

What retirement portfolio looks like: (100% = $16,000)

His 401k account has only this one fund:

 100% VASGX Vanguard LifeStrategy Growth Fund, ER 0.17%

  The fund maintains this fixed allocation:

  o *56% Vanguard Total Stock Market Index Fund*
  o *24% Vanguard Total International Stock Index Fund*
  o *20% Vanguard Total Bond Market Index Fund*

What other investments look like:

- Emergency Fund: (4 months expenses) in intermediate-term Treasury fund in his Roth IRA account. Bonds are for low risk. His contributions could be withdrawn in an emergency. Bond interest is not taxed in this account.
- Other saving: $7,000 in a taxable Vanguard account targeted for spending in the next several years (house down-payment, vacations). For this purpose, he uses a short-term Treasury fund for very low risk because he fully expects to use this money.

110

New annual contributions:

- $4,000 to his 401k (plus employer match up to $4,000) plus half of all future raises.
- $6,000 to his taxable account

What Simon Simple knows about himself:

- The automatically-rebalanced, all-in-one-fund portfolio will eliminate temptation to tinker with the asset allocation.
- He appreciates simplicity—no rebalancing computations.
- Plans to shift towards bonds closer to retirement.
- Bought a used car with cash and plans to drive it many years.
- He pays all credit cards fully, and on-time.
- He currently saves 10% of his gross income towards retirement but is committed to contributing half of everything he earns over $40,000 to this account (i.e., half of all raises), because he won't miss what he never had.

Rick's assessment and commentary about Simple's portfolio:

- ✓ Bond allocation is appropriate
- ✓ There's a workable plan
- ✓ Stocks are highly diversified
- ✓ Investments are low-cost
- ✓ Uses tax-advantaged accounts
- ✓ Easy to manage
- ✓ Debt management
- ✓ Continuous contributions
- ✓ On track for their goals

Key point: Simplicity is underappreciated. One fund can be fine. Most everyone can do this themselves!

Key point: Both Vanguard's LifeStrategy and Target Retirement fund families are stellar for their low-cost and simplicity and provide excellent benchmarks to compare other choices to.

Youngs, ages 32, married, 70/30,   ★★★★★

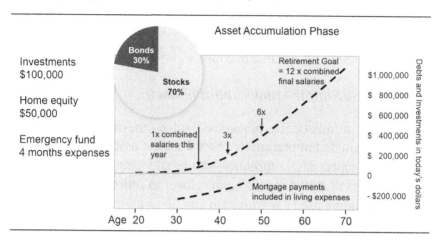

Investments
$100,000

Home equity
$50,000

Emergency fund
4 months expenses

What retirement portfolio looks like: (100% = $100,000)

Their taxable accounts at Fidelity:

- 7% FSTVX Spartan Total US Market Index, ER 0.05%
- 7% FSIVX Fidelity Spartan Int'l Equity Index, ER 0.12%

His 401k at Fidelity

- 7% FSTVX Spartan Total US Market Index, ER 0.05%
- 7% FSIVX Fidelity Spartan Int'l Equity Index, ER 0.12%
- 15% 10-yr Treasury bonds, purchased at auction, no costs.

Her IRA at Fidelity

- 7% FSTVX Spartan Total US Market Index, ER 0.05%
- 7% FSIVX Fidelity Spartan Int'l Equity Index, ER 0.12%
- 15% FIBAX Spartan Intermed Treas Bond Index, ER 0.10%

His Roth IRA at Fidelity

- 14% FSTVX Spartan Total US Market Index, ER 0.05%

Her Roth IRA at Fidelity

- 14% FSIVX Fidelity Spartan Int'l Equity Index, ER 0.12%

What other investments look like:

- Emergency Fund: $12,000 in online bank account at 1%
- Home equity: $50,000

New annual contributions:

- $5,000 to his 401k (plus a $4,000 employer match)
- $5,000 to her 401k
- $3,000 to his Roth IRA
- $3,000 to her Roth IRA

What the Young family knows about themselves:

- They further allocate stocks: 1/2 international and 1/2 U.S.
- Plan to gradually shift to more bonds each year.
- They buy used cars with cash and drive them many years.
- They pay their credit cards fully, and on-time.
- They save 15% of their gross income towards retirement plus another 5% towards shorter-term big-ticket items.

Rick's assessment and commentary about their portfolio:

✓ Bond allocation is appropriate
✓ There's a workable plan
✓ Stocks are highly diversified
✓ Investments are low-cost
✓ Uses tax-advantaged accounts
✓ Easy to manage
✓ Debt management
✓ Continuous contributions (automatic from paycheck)
✓ On-track for their goals

Key point: The Fidelity Spartan family of funds are stellar low-cost alternatives to consider or compare to.

Key point: This is a 3-fund portfolio. There are a hundred other portfolios that may be equally good—you can't know which will be "best of the best" in advance. The key is to choose a coherent low-cost plan that matches your goals—and then stick to it!

Larry, age 45, single, 100% Stocks,

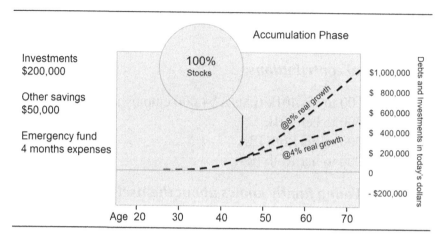

What retirement portfolio looks like: (100% = $200,000)

His taxable accounts (this portion allocated for retirement):

- 60% in five individual stocks, small broker fees
- 5% in cash (money market fund)

His 401k at Fidelity:

- 35% FSTVX Spartan Total US Market Index, ER 0.05%

What other investments look like:

- Emergency Fund: Larry is using his large taxable account for this and mentally allocates 1/3 of it to spend on big-ticket items in the near to mid-term future.

New annual contributions:

He had been contributing less. Here's his new plan:

- $6,000 to his 401k (plus employer matches first $4,000)
- $10,000 to his taxable account.

What Larry Latecomer thinks about himself:

- Chooses the extra risk of being 100% in stocks to make up

for starting late.

- His taxable account (stocks) is also his emergency fund.
- Only invests in proven performers (impressive track record, a 5-star Morningstar rating, and endorsement of his broker)
- He now saves 15% of his gross income towards retirement.

Rick's assessment and commentary about Larry's portfolio:

Unlike Dr. Frugal's portfolio, this 100% stock portfolio is likely to cause trouble for Larry. He had little invested during the severe bear market in 2008 so his behavior is untested. His strategy chases after yesterday's winners (tomorrow's losers?) and will not capture tomorrow's winners. Worse, stuff happens and his emergency fund is in stocks. He might have to sell into a bear market. Larry needs a plan for when and how to get to an appropriate allocation to bonds.

✗ Bond allocation is appropriate? *No. too little, too risky.*
✓ There's a workable plan? *Partly; if sticks to saving enough.*
✗ Stocks are highly diversified? *No, uncompensated risk.*
✓ Investments are low-cost
✗ Uses tax-advantaged accounts? *Missing advantages here.*
✗ Easy to manage? *No, he likely tracks these stocks daily.*
✗ Debt management? *Don't see signs of being frugal here.*
✓ Continuous contributions? *Good. Auto payroll deductions.*
✗ On-track for their goals? *Close, with adjustments*

There is a big problem balancing and diversifying a portfolio like this without incurring taxable gains, but this should be explored to diversify the taxable account. Emphasis should be placed on putting new contributions in tax-deferred account(s)—both for the tax advantages and for the ease of rebalancing and maintaining a chosen level of risk. Less important, but I also recommend diversifying internationally with between 20 and 50% of the stocks.

Key point: Increasing investment risk is not a substitute for starting to save earlier. Plus, owning individual stocks is accepting additional risk that is uncompensated by the stock market. Larry needs to stick to his new aggressive saving rate, and explore how to diversify and take advantage of tax-advantaged accounts. Now.

115

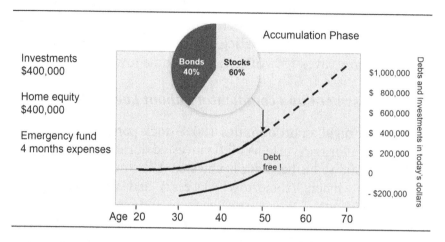

What retirement portfolio looks like: (100% = $400,000)

His 401k account, expensive funds (but front-end loads waived)

- 14% in American Bond Fund, annual cost 1.17%
- 12% in American Stock Growth Fund, annual cost 1.17%

In identical Roth accounts for each of them at Vanguard:

- 74% VTWNX Vanguard Target Retirement Fnd, ER 0.16% (This is broadly diversified, but 65% stocks)

What other investments look like:

- Emergency Fund: $20,000 FDIC-insured CDs (online bank).
- Home equity: $400,000
- Short-term targeted spending: $120,000 in FDIC-insured high-yield online bank CDs targeted for spending in the next several years (for next car and children's college).

New annual contributions:

- $4,000 his 401k (plus company will match up to $4,000)
- $6,500 to her Roth IRA account.
- $6,500 to his Roth IRA account.

116

What M.T. Nesters know about themselves:

- He doesn't have good low-cost fund choices in his 401k but contributes the minimum to get the company match.
- They appreciate simplicity.
- They buy used cars with cash and drive them many years.
- They pay their credit cards fully, and on-time.
- They save 10% of their gross income towards retirement plus another 5% towards shorter-term big-ticket items.

Rick's assessment and commentary about their portfolio:

It's good to use a company retirement plan to get automatic payroll deductions. This is invaluable for getting into the habit of saving without thinking about it. But it is especially important to take advantage of plans that include an employer match.

The M.T. Nesters are doing the best possible in their situation which includes a 401k with only bad (expensive) fund options. So, for doing a great job with the choices they can control, I'll give it a qualified 5-stars.

- ✓ Bond allocation is appropriate
- ✓ There's a workable plan
- ✓ Stocks are highly diversified
- – Investments are low-cost? *It's mostly excellent; best possible.*
- ✓ Uses tax-advantaged accounts
- ✓ Easy to manage
- ✓ Debt management
- ✓ Continuous contributions
- ✓ On-track for their goals

Key point: If your 401k only has poor fund choices, use it to get the company match, then use an IRA of your own. Later, roll your bad 401k to a self-managed IRA after you leave the company.

Lonny & Lola, age 60, married, 50/50 ★★★★★

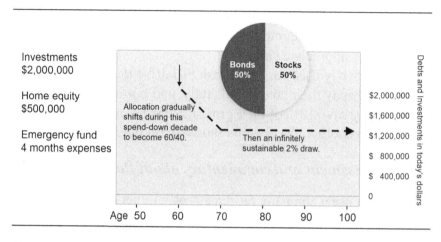

Investments
$2,000,000

Home equity
$500,000

Emergency fund
4 months expenses

Bonds 50%   Stocks 50%

Allocation gradually shifts during this spend-down decade to become 60/40.

Then an infinitely sustainable 2% draw.

Debts and Investments in today's dollars

$2,000,000
$1,600,000
$1,200,000
$ 800,000
$ 400,000
0

Age 50   60   70   80   90   100

What retirement portfolio looks like: (100% = $2,000,000)

Their taxable account at Fidelity:

- 7% VEU Vanguard Int'l Equity Index ETF, ER 0.15%

His Rollover IRA:

- 25% in Individual TIPs, no costs.
- 10% FSTVX Spartan Total US Market Index, ER 0.05%

Her Rollover IRA:

- 25% in FDIC-insured high-yield 5-year CDs, no costs.
- 5% FSIVX Fidelity Spartan Int'l Equity Index, ER 0.12
- 10% VBR Vanguard Small-Value Index ETF, ER 0.09%

They both have identical Roths IRAs which combined look like:

- 13% FSTVX Spartan Total US Market Index, ER 0.05%
- 5% FSIVX Spartan Int'l Equity Index, ER 0.12%

What other investments look like:

- Home Equity: $500,000
- Emerg fund is in an FDIC-insured high-yield online bank.

What Lonny and Lola know about themselves:

- Retiring this year but both plan to defer full Social Security until age 70.
- Must draw $80,000 for next ten years so this is a conservative 50/50 portfolio. Thereafter, plan to draw $25,000+ from their investments with a 60/40 portfolio.
- They appreciate simplicity.

Rick's assessment and commentary about their portfolio:

✓ Bond allocation is appropriate
✓ There's a workable plan
✓ Stocks are highly diversified
✓ Investments are low-cost
✓ Uses tax-advantaged accounts
✓ Easy to manage
✓ Debt management
~~Continuous contributions~~ (none; retired)
✓ On-track for their goals

Key point: This is a very low cost portfolio. The cost of the bond portion is zero—could not be lower. The stock funds also low-cost.

Key point: This portfolio is an example of removing market risk after reaching your investment goal. Think that is easy during a bull market? Well it is for this couple who are now out of the workforce.

Key point: The bond portion of this portfolio has eliminated all credit risk by using exclusively treasury bonds (TIPS) and FDIC-insured CDs. Such extremes are not necessary, but this book does advocate keeping your investment risks on the stock side of your portfolio.

Key point: They recognize the huge advantage of each postponing Social Security to age 70 to achieve a high inflation-adjusted lifetime annuity.

Al & Shill Pay, ages 70, married, 80/20 ★★ ★ ★ ★

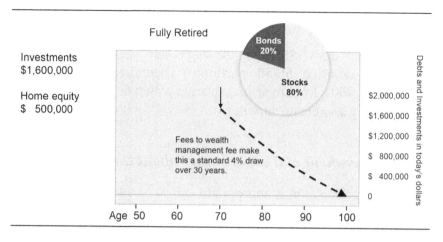

What retirement portfolio looks like: (100% = $1,600,000)

Their taxable account:

- 5% cash for current living expenses

His Rollover IRA at a giant wealth management firm for 1.25% / yr.

- 40% in seventy selected individual stocks
- 10% in selected individual bonds

Her Rollover IRA at giant wealth management firm for 1.25% / yr.

- 40% in seventy selected individual stocks
- 5% in selected individual bonds

What other investments look like:

- $500,000 equity in their home.

What Al and Shill Pay think about themselves:

- Our retirement portfolio is twice as large as we need, so we keep the $800K retirement portion at 60% stocks and 40% bonds, but allocate the remaining legacy portion of $800K to be 100% stocks.

- The combination of the large legacy portion, and our low draw (2.75% of the total each year), allow us to take above normal (for our age) risk.

Rick's assessment and commentary about their portfolio:

This is a portfolio of managed stocks and in this sense it is difficult to distinguish it from countless expensive actively-managed funds. Clients typically justify paying the high fee after hearing a sales pitch that the firm is able to predict bull markets and can move you out of the market in advance. So, why bother with bonds?

Well, it is worse than it looks. There are cases where wealthy individuals might reasonably choose more risk for the legacy portion of their portfolio, but this is NOT one of those examples.

A stock portfolio is very sensitive to a series of bad returns early on in retirement. It would be true that this portfolio is somewhat less vulnerable to failure if the annual draw was only of 2.75% ($44K/yr), but they are ignoring the management fee which is another $20K/yr. That's right! They are actually drawing 4% from their investments, and paying a third of that to the management company. Is that fair? Is the firm adding commensurate value?

Key point: A 4% draw has a very high risk of being depleted in 30 years—same as giving the legacy portion to the management firm!

Is this highway robbery, or just the delusion that smart people can play the stock market and achieve higher returns that justify the costs? Index funds are superior and ten times less expensive.

Key point: You get to keep what you don't have to pay as fees.

I would prefer to see this couple designate $500K as an intended legacy portion and invest it in the total stock market as low-cost as possible. Then, a 4% draw of the balance would give them $44K that increases with inflation to fund their needs for the next 30 years—and this portion should be invested conservatively and as low-cost as possible.

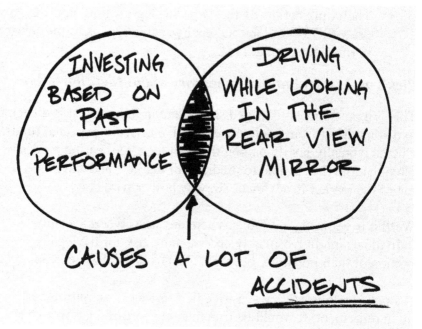

Sketch by Carl Richards at BehaviorGap.com

Common Misconceptions Important to Correct

Sadly, this is an industry where common sense is drowned-out. It is difficult for investors to let wisdom in and keep the noise out. The noise comes from people who have something to sell you.

Financial news (television) channels are selling their audience's attention to advertisers. The audience includes investors who hope they will hear a tip about how to "beat the market."

Investing professionals are selling investment services. Too often they seem to be trying to convince us how complex the finance world is, and how they are uniquely situated to sell us valuable advice.

Newsletters are selling subscriptions to investors who think they can buy knowledge that can be used to "beat the market."

Finance magazines are similar, plus they sell their readers' attention to advertisers.

Fund companies are competing with each other for your investment dollars which generate income through fees called "expense ratio," sales commissions, broker fees, annual account fees, and others.

Many book authors feed on our greed. The same base instincts that drive people to buy lottery tickets also drive them to buy books about how to *beat the market.*

It is hard to make wise decisions if you cannot understand the motives behind your information sources. If you cannot identify conflicts of interest, you should keep asking questions until you are satisfied.

All of the following pages are widespread misconceptions—usually attributable to wishful thinking, but sometimes encouraged by a misguided sales pitch.

Stocks Are Safer In The Long Run

TRUTH: *Our measure of uncertainty and volatility, the standard deviation of the <u>total return</u>, actually <u>increases</u> with time horizon.*

John Norstad wrote an excellent paper[55] showing that time does not reduce equity risk; it increases it. In other words, the range of outcomes from your long-term stock investments is bigger, and remain bigger, than you might expect. Here's an example of how it works in simple terms followed by a link to his paper.

In my first book, *Common Sense Investing*, I showed two pictures of annualized total returns for large company stocks from date to date. Each bar in the first picture is the annualized returns from holding the stocks for one year. The stock market looks impressively volatile, just as we experience it. The second picture considers the annualized return when the stocks are held for ten years. These thumbnail pictures will remind you:

Large Company Stocks 1926 thru 2008

One-Year Returns	Annualized Ten-Year Returns

The Annualized Ten-Year Returns are the rates that if constant year-after-year for ten years would produce the same ten-year outcomes. It's rarely negative and never by much. However, this masks the fact that it is often a wild ride.

Norstad asserts that many investors look at this and mistakenly conclude, "Give me enough time for all those ups and downs in the market to even out and I can't lose!"[56]

"The longer you hold stocks, the less your risk and the surer your gain," writes Charles Ellis, one of my favorite authors.[57]

Another variation of this argument is to show how annualized variability decreases with time. Mr. Bogle uses this compelling metric to reinforce his point that focusing on the long term is far superior to focusing on the short term. Vanguard depicts is graphically, like this:[58]

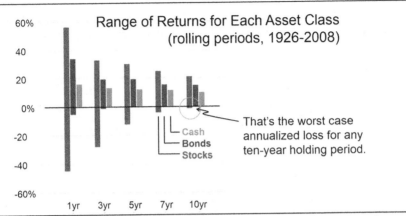

Here is another common way that people are mislead into thinking that stock-market risk decreases as holding periods increase.

While true, it's not what we care about. We care about our total return, and when we compound the variability over time we see that this range of outcomes *increases* with longer time horizons.

This basic argument that the standard deviations of the *annualized returns* decrease as the time horizon increases is true but "fatally misses the point," because for an investor concerned with the value of his portfolio at the end of a period of time, it is the *total return* that matters, not the *annualized return*.

If we apply our intuition we know that Norstad is correct. We are always subject to the full wrath of the stock market—it doesn't know or care when we purchased the stock! That's why our rule of thumb is that our stock portion of our portfolios might lose 1/2 its value in *any* year.

Norstad's paper is eminently readable, brilliant, and compelling for those who need further persuasion. He shows that "because of the effects of compounding, the standard deviation of the *total return* actually increases with time horizon. Thus, if we use the traditional measure of uncertainty as the standard deviation of return over the time period in question, uncertainty increases with time horizon."

125

Norstad shines a bright light on the popular notion that stock investing over long periods of time is safe because good and bad returns will somehow "even out over time." Not only is this common opinion false, it is dangerous—in that it down plays the real risk in stock investing. It's risk that most of us accept because it is accompanied by the potential for great rewards, but we must not ignore the risk.

A Better Chart Showing Risk Over Time

This chart clearly shows the dramatic increasing uncertainty of an S&P 500 stock investment as time horizon increases. Look at the enormous range of outcomes.

Norstad's chart shows the growth of a $1000 investment in a statistical model of the S&P 500 stock market index over time horizons ranging from 1 to 40 years. It pretty much speaks for itself, and he interprets like this:

> The chart clearly shows the dramatic increasing uncertainty of an S&P 500 stock investment as time horizon increases. For example, at 40 years, the chart gives only a 2 in 3 chance that the ending value will be somewhere between $14,000 and $166,000. This is an enormous range of possible outcomes, and there's a significant 1 in 3 chance that the actual ending value will be below or above the range! You can't get much more uncertain than this.

As long as we're talking about risk, let's consider a really bad case. If instead of investing our $1000 in the S&P 500, we put it in a bank earning 6% interest, after 40 years we'd have $10,286. This is 1.26 standard deviations below the median ending value of the S&P 500 investment. The probability of ending up below this point is 10%. In other words, even over a very long 40 year time horizon, we still have about a 1 in 10 chance of ending up with less money than if we had put it in the bank!

If you look at just the median values in isolation, you see the familiar geometric growth you get with the magic of compounding. But without showing the other possible outcomes and their ranges it suggests certainty that is fantasy. When you're doing financial planning, it's extremely important to look at *both* return *and* risk.

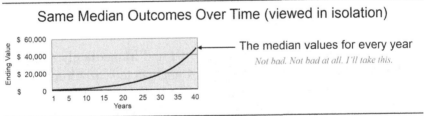

There is a 1 in 2 chance for an outcome above the median, and the same chance for ending below. Viewing in isolation hides the enormous range of possible outcomes.

Many academics, but not all, believe that the market exhibits a phenomenon called "reversion to the mean." While this decreases the standard deviations on his pure random walk model at longer time horizons, it does not change his basic conclusion that the uncertainty of the ending values *increases with time*.

Norstad's paper can be found here:

www.norstad.org/finance/risk-and-time.html

Holding a Bond (or CD) to Maturity Eliminates Risk

All bonds are subject to interest-rate risk.

No interest rate risk if you get your investment back at maturity—right? Nope, another widely-held myth. Earlier in this book we used this example from author Allan Roth which he told as follows: [59]

> As it turns out, the argument that holding a bond to maturity eliminates interest rate risk is completely false. Let's look at this example:
>
> You buy a one-year bond today for $1,000 that promises to pay back $1,050 in one year. The interest rate is 5 percent ($1,050 - $1,000)/$1,000. The value of the bond today is $1,000, calculated as follows:
>
> 1,050/1.05 = $1,000
>
> Your luck happened to be really bad and immediately after buying this bond, the CPI showed unexpected inflation and interest rates shot up. Seconds after buying this bond, the same bond is now yielding 6 percent. A new bond would now be paying $1,060 in a year. The bond you bought, however, is giving you back only $1,050, so now the value of your bond is calculated as follows:
>
> 1,050/1.06 = $990.57
>
> Or, a decline of $9.43 from the $1,000 you paid.
>
> Because interest rates went up by 1 percent, the value of your bond dropped by $9.43 or 0.94 percent. If you keep the bond for the entire year, you'll get $1,050 back and won't have the loss, right? Well, not so fast. Remember that the new bond is paying 6 percent, so you missed out on buying the $1,000 bond that would have paid $1,060, or an additional $10.00. So, holding onto the bond has an *opportunity cost* of $10.00 which is currently worth:
>
> $10/1.06 = $9.43

It's no accident that the decline in value is exactly equal to your opportunity cost of holding it to maturity. Bond markets are extremely efficient. Holding a bond to maturity, even in a laddered portfolio, provides no protection from interest rate risk.

Key Point: All bonds, including CDs, are subject to interest-rate risk, even though you get back the principal (par value) on the date promised just like agreed to when purchased the bond.

This was a good enough deal when you took it yesterday! What was the risk? You lost the opportunity to gain even more interest by investing your cash a day later at the new higher interest rate. But if you kept your money in a money market attempting to guess what will happen to interest rates then you also have the opportunity cost from having your money out of the market.

Heads-up! Many professionals get this wrong. If your investment advisor tries to sell you individual bonds, or a bond ladder, as a way to eliminate interest rate risk, head for the door!

"But wait," you think. "CDs are an exception! Their price doesn't decline when the interest rate rises—so, no interest rate risk." Not so. Just because a bank-issued CD is not marketable does not mean its value doesn't change. When interest rates rise, the CD is worth less by exactly the opportunity cost of that money being invested at the higher rate. For the case of a CD, the opportunity cost includes the "early withdrawal penalty" for redeeming and reinvesting the CD at the new higher rate.

Stocks Are Safer Than Bonds

TRUTH: *As usual, it depends—upon how you define risk. Stocks and bonds play different roles in your portfolio. You need to harness their unique attributes to help you achieve your financial goals.*

Don't settle for a simple answer only to miss the point. But this argument is to miss the point. The purpose for bonds is as a riskless ballast to your portfolio—a ready reserve for emergencies, for those stocks or real estate that you want to be ready for.

Stocks more risky than bonds?

If you consider risk to be short-term market fluctuations, then we can conclude that stocks are riskier than bonds. This is exactly what we want to consider as our needs for the money approach in time.

But, as mentioned earlier, long-term investors can safely ignore short-term volatility. So since stocks, unlike bonds, don't guarantee a rate-of-return, the risk for the long-term investor is that stock returns will be terrible.

Norstad reminds us that the range of potential outcomes actually increases with time, so the need to become more conservative as you approach your needs for money requires annual intervention to handle this gradually with your stock/bond allocation

Stocks Can Be Less Risky Than Bonds

But if the goal of a long-term investor is real, inflation-adjusted growth, then we must use a different metric to look at real returns, or inflation-adjusted returns. John C. Bogle, legendary founder of Vanguard, puts it this way in his book *Common Sense on Mutual Funds*: "The data make clear that, if risk is the chance of failing to earn a real return over the long term, bonds have carried a higher risk than stock."

To me, this argues in favor of starting to save and invest early and gradually increasing your allocation in bonds as you approach retirement.

The Best Funds Have The Most Stars

TRUTH: *The best funds are those that are widely diversified at the lowest cost.*

The best funds have these attributes that can be measured:

- Closely track a benchmark index

- Low transaction costs and operating expenses

- Tax efficient (low turnover)

Each of these drive out costs. The direct costs are the most obvious to investors, and include broker fees (for ETFs), sales commissions (also called "loads"), and the expense ratio. Less obvious are the costs that you must pay as income taxes that are not deferred. These are incurred because of active trading, or *turnover*. And lastly are the unintended costs or human errors attributable to active investing.

It used to be that recent winners would get rated highly. This was problematic because, if index funds are the benchmark, there will always be some funds that over-performed (5-stars?) while the index funds represent the average (3-stars?). Very often, yesterday's winners become tomorrow's losers, while average stays average. It's not like school where average implies mediocre. It is **difficult** to achieving the index benchmark return because of costs. (Beware of comparing to a fund containing stocks of higher risk.)

In 2012 Morningstar tried to address the backward-looking limitations of the "star rating" system and reduce its bias to recent history by adding a forward-looking analyst rating of Gold, Silver, or Bronze—but the predictive power of analysts has never been very reliable either.

Instead of relying on Morningstar or anyone else to help you select outperforming funds, you should shift your focus to *capturing the returns of the total worldwide market* by using funds with the lowest costs. This is hardly news. In 1966, the economist William Sharpe stated, "all other things being equal, the smaller a fund's expense ratio, the better results obtained by its stock holders."

131

A One Percent Fee Is Small

TRUTH: *"In investing, you get what you don't pay for."*
– John C. Bogle

One percent may be small compared to 100%. But earning 5% and then giving away 1% as a fee is huge—it's one-fifth of your earnings, and some years much more.

The common assumption is that investors will get compensated for the fees with higher returns. Yet, the overwhelming evidence is that fees don't help you to *beat* the market. So the issue becomes: do you personally need to pay an advisor a management fee in order to earn the market return?

Would you like to know the easiest way to increase your wealth by 33% in the next thirty years? You guessed it! Simply reduce your investment fees by one percent.

Proof for a typical *conservative* investment portfolio which achieves average return of 3.5% after management fees and fund expenses.

Total return for the stocks and bonds *before fees* = 5%.

Value of $10,000 invested 30 years with fees totaling 1.5% /yr:
$10,000 (1.035)^30 = $24,273.

Value of $10,000 invested 30 years with fees totaling 0.5% /yr:
$10,000 (1.045)^30 = $32,434 (33% larger!)

But wait. It's even worse when you're in retirement with a larger portfolio and no new income! Remember Dr. Clever who is drawing $40,000 each year from a $1 million portfolio that is similar to this? He decides to use a large full-service brokerage and pays the typical 1.0% in advisory fees plus another 0.5% in additional brokerage/service fees, which is common. But that's 1.5% of all he owns, which equals $15,000 per year. So every year, on top of the $40,000 he takes out to spend, another $15,000— or 38% more—is lost to unnecessarily high expenses.[60]

A life-changing sentence that drove this home for me was John

Bogle saying the obvious: that we get to keep what we don't give away in costs of all types.

Bonus: If you accomplish this by switching to low-cost index funds then you can accomplish this outstanding bonus return for no additional investment risk! How many opportunities do you get to do that?

The way to make this happen is to become keenly aware of the fees you are paying. The ways you become keenly aware are:

(1) Constantly ask yourself, "How does this service provider get paid?" In other words, if this isn't explicit then it is happening through hidden fees and spreads. Don't kid yourself—this is taken out of what you earn. You just get the net amount after fees. Always.

(2) Convert all these fee percentages to actual dollars, then ask yourself whether you are getting good value. For instance, are you paying somebody 1% to manage your $200,000 portfolio? Is $2,000 per year a fair amount for the service? Often it is cheaper to pay fixed amounts for specific one-time services than to pay these annual fees.

(3) Develop radar for recognizing conflicts of interest. Go ahead and ask how they get compensated for selling you particular products.

Notice that while I myself am an ardent do-it-yourselfer, I am NOT requiring this of any of you. Instead, I am proposing you simply get educated. Decide what services you might want, and don't pay for services you don't want or need.

"But one percent is well worth it if I earn more than that."

If you believe this, you took their bait. You've been sold. Well—it might be worth it if you are certain that you are an emotional klutz and cannot trust yourself to stick with a plan. That's not you! A little education might be the best investment you ever make.

Go read about active investing. The vast weight of evidence is against this. Identify *all* your costs. Ultimately passive investing with index funds prevails. *It's because of the lower costs.*

Rising Interest Rates are Bad for Bond Holders

TRUTH: *Ultimately rising rates are good for bond holders because they can reinvest their coupons (interest payments) at the new higher rates. In the short term they are a little bit bad (nothing compared to stock market volatility) and even this disappears if the bond or bond fund is held longer than the time called "duration" after an interest rate increase.*

Low interest rates, and the prospects of rising interest rates, are the two main reasons investors have reluctance to include the correct amount of bonds in their portfolio.

We cannot invest in yesterday's bonds—only what is available at today's interest rates. Don't be overly concerned about rising interest rates.

Recall that "duration" is the point of indifference to interest rate changes. If you own the bonds for longer than the duration (years) after an interest rate increase and reinvest the coupon interest, then you will be ahead of where you were when you purchased because of the higher interest rates.

I don't believe we can forecast future interest rates any better than we can foretell the stock market, so I hold short- and intermediate-term bonds, and TIPs at all maturities. But, if you are convinced that interest rates are going to rise, then simply choose a high-grade bond fund with short duration, or a short-term individual bond or CD which have durations that decrease automatically. The price you pay for interest rate immunity is lower yields.

It is actually *real* interest rates that matter—investment growth after adjusting for inflation. You might review how TIPS can protect you from inflation being higher than expected.

You Can't Beat the Market Using Index Funds

TRUTH: *This, of course, is true. You can't __beat__ the market using index funds because index funds try to reflect, or track the market. But more importantly, the probability is much lower using actively managed funds—mostly because of their costs.*

Usually this argument comes at you along the lines of: "You don't want to be average, do you?" There might be a subtle pitch to go with an investment company (or advisor) because they have the research teams and access or tools to choose stocks and bonds better than average. And it seems plausible to you. The smarter students were always better than *average*! It seems plausible that they should be able to select stocks that perform "above average."

Well no. Lose that thought! The more important truth is that the probability of underperforming the market is higher with actively managed funds. On average they underperform by the amount of their fees and expenses. Studies show that 63% underperform every year, rising to 85% underperforming after 10 years, then 95% underperforming after 25 years.[61]

Marketing departments are adept at conflating this—comparing their fund to some popular standard that isn't equivalent risk. For example, how should you feel about their "Aggressive Stock Fund that outperforms S&P500 by 10%"?

Well, now we have an apples-to-oranges comparison. It is perfectly fair to add risk to your portfolio to create a higher expected return. A smart way to do this would be to exchange a little of your total market fund for an asset class like a small-cap value index fund. But never lose sight that you are choosing more risk than the market portfolio. Actively managed funds are rarely the way to do this, and it is mostly (but not entirely) due to the higher fees they charge.

Use Multiple Investment Companies To Diversify

TRUTH: *Virtually all your risk is in the companies that issue the stocks and bonds you hold.*

Virtually all your risk is in the companies that issue the stocks and bonds you hold, not the companies holding the assets for you.

These are your assets, and investment services companies hold them in segregated custodian accounts. Federal laws keep the fund securities isolated from any potential claims against the custodians.

I personally find high value in simplicity, although there is no problem if your company's 401(k) is with Fidelity, your Roth IRA is with Vanguard, and your emergency fund is in a CD in an online bank.

However, if you have half a dozen other investment firms then it could be that you misunderstand the essence of diversifying the investment assets themselves. Most importantly, this sort of unfocused approach (1) complicates your life and managing your investments, (2) potentially keeps you out of some cheaper funds that are available with larger investments—the admiral shares at Vanguard, or the advantage shares at Fidelity, and (3) to some extent you may be paying account service charges, or small balance fees.

If you would like to learn more, I suggest your next stop should be this blog article. Mike Piper is the author of this blog. He is a CPA and the author of several personal finance books. The point of this blog is to show that investing doesn't have to be complicated. I read it weekly and highly recommend it.

http://www.obliviousinvestor.com/is-it-safer-to-use-multiple-fund-companies/

You Need Many Mutual Funds to Diversify

TRUTH: *You can have an excellent portfolio with a single mutual fund if you choose one that is broadly diversified and low-cost.*

Unless you have a specific reason why you want to take on additional risk for a higher expected return, then stay with simple! A total U.S. market index fund contains thousands of stocks/bonds weighted to their market capitalization. This means that the companies get represented in the index fund in proportion to their size—as they should.

An example of a specific reason to own more than one fund would be to diversify internationally—but here again, you can accomplish that with a single fund. The last chapter in this book illustrates some examples of mixed-asset funds which give you more diversification at very low cost.

Sometimes there is an identical version of a fund available for larger investments with lower costs (called *expense ratio*) which directly enhances your return. For example, at Vanguard these are called *Admiral* shares of a fund (> $10,000) and at Fidelity these are called *Advantage* shares (also for $10,000 minimum investments).

One reason to own additional funds could also be to overweight part of the market to seek both higher-risk and expected returns. But while investors have been rewarded for taking the extra risks of "small stocks" and "value stocks," as well as for taking "bond term" risk, they have received almost no reward for accepting *credit* risks.

The "bond term" premium is significant for U.S. Treasuries, and many investors find intermediate-term bonds provide a good balance between the risks of interest rate changes and inflation.

However, the "bond default" risk is an anomaly. So, bond experts like Larry Swedroe generally advise against seeking higher bond yields from foreign, emerging market bond, or high-yield bonds, and instead to take your risk on the stock side of your portfolio where you generally get a better return for the risk that you choose.[62]

Frugal Means *Cheap*; *Stingy*; *Miserly*; *Tightwad.*

TRUTH: *Frugality is all about enjoying, not penny pinching.*

Everybody knows a *cheap* person, and probably hates them. But we often mislabel *frugal* people as cheap. Cheap and frugal people both love to save money, but here are some differences:[63]

1. Frugal people will not do so at the expense of others.
2. Cheapness uses price as a bottom line; frugality uses value as a bottom line.
3. Cheap people are driven by saving money regardless of the cost; frugal people are driven by maximizing total value, including the value of their time.
4. Being cheap is about spending less; being frugal is about prioritizing your spending so that you can have more of the things you really care about.

I am proud to be frugal. I consider it a virtue. Here is why I discuss it in this book.

There is great power in this truth: We each will get a certain number of heart beats during our lifetime—we just don't know how many. Author Vicki Robin has a very practical concept that is similar— that our lifetimes each have an amount of "life energy" that we can largely allocate as we choose.[64] Of key interest is the life energy we trade for money when we have a job. When you add up and become conscious of all the life energy you invest in a job to bring home $1,000, it makes you think very carefully about spending it in manner that will bring you the most joy.

She writes that ultimately, *you* are the one who determines what money is worth *to you*. It is *your* life energy. You *pay* for money with your time. You choose how to spend it. Sure, some of it is necessarily spent sleeping, eating, washing and exercising, but you can spend your remaining life energy for such discretionary uses as:

- your relationship to yourself
- your relationship to others
- your creative expression

- your contribution to your community
- your contribution to the world
- achieving inner peace and . . .
- holding down a job

Frugal people know that money is something you trade life energy for and they prioritize how they use that valuable commodity. After all, is there any *thing* more vital to you than your life energy?

Frugal people understand that they can get far more enjoyment from saving hard earned money and spending it carefully, than by working harder or longer to buy things we only marginally value.

Author Andrew Tobias changed my life as a young man by writing:[65]

A Penny Saved Is Two Pennies Earned.

Most people are in a higher tax bracket than they realize. If you wish to figure it out, consider how much you would pay if you were earned an additional $1,000. You might pay an additional 25% (or more) in federal income taxes, plus payroll taxes (Social Security and Medicare)—which is even more if you are self-employed, plus state and local taxes. It adds up! Most people will only get to keep one-half to two-thirds of these earnings.

Allan Roth points out in the following example[66] that while earning more is always good, it actually has a far lower impact on years of financial freedom than spending less.

> As an example, let's say that a 50-year-old can make $10,000 a year more and will retire in 15 years, which translates to $150,000. But if a third goes to taxes, he is left with only an additional $100,000. On the other hand, if he spends $10,000 a year less and has a 33-year life expectancy, that translates to $330,000 in savings.

> In the above example, lowering annual expenditures by $10,000 had an approximately 3.3-fold benefit over earning $10,000 more. That means **a dollar saved is worth far more than a dollar earned**; in the example, it equaled approximately $3.30.

139

The frugal lifestyle is about getting maximum enjoyment from the things you do choose spend money on. People with a frugal lifestyle are most apt to achieve their other goals through aggressively saving, investing wisely, and then consciously spending.

The marginal enjoyment from the bigger car, the bigger boat, the newest gadgets, has diminishing return. It ultimately means investing more time at your job, investing more of your life energy to pay for it. It keeps you from saving and investing adequately to eventually achieve financial freedom—where you can wake up every morning and spend your life energy on the projects that are of interest *to you*.

At what age will you wake up every morning with that kind of freedom—instead of having to work to pay the bills? That's my idea of *financial independence*. Money plays an important role, but so does the lifestyle you choose.

Key point: The frugal person gets the double bonus of saving more and using their savings for longer.

The frugal person can achieve financial independence more easily, and choose to spend the rest of their life in service to others—or, however they choose. It's the shortest path to financial independence where you can have the freedom to spend your time as you enjoy.

"We investors as a group get precisely what we don't pay for. So if we pay nothing, we get everything."

—John C. Bogle

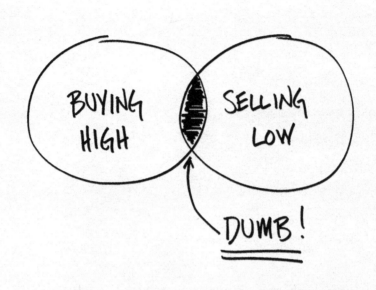

Sketch by Carl Richards at BehaviorGap.com

This brilliant sketch by Carl Richards succinctly sums up the point of this book: the greatest protection you have from yourself is to own the correct amount of low-risk assets with payouts that match your needs.

Notes

[1] This chart was created by Professor Jeremy Siegel, Professor of Finance at the Wharton School of the University of Pennsylvania. Used with permission.

[2] John C. Bogle takes the nominal returns in this chart and converts them to real returns in Common Sense on Mutual Funds, 1999, page 8.

[3] This chart from Fidelity.com is called Hypothetical Growth of $10,000 for FSTVX, which is a low-cost mutual fund for the Total U.S. Stock Market. It is a standard way to illustrate total return over time.

[4] Dr. William Bernstein quote from
http://www.efficientfrontier.com/ef/997/maturity.htm

[5] Author Larry Swedroe makes the point that correlation between high-yield bonds with stocks shows up at exactly the wrong times. Here are three references from his book "The Only Guide To A Winning Bond Strategy You'll Ever Need":

"Given that a high (if not the highest) priority for investors, whether in the accumulation or withdrawal stage, is safety or stability of principal, the prudent choice is to restrict holdings to only the two highest investment grades, AAA and AA. One of the major reasons is that as the credit rating decreases, the correlation with equity returns increases. This is a strong negative feature of lower-rated bonds—they are more likely than higher-rated bonds to perform poorly at the same time that stocks are performing poorly." (p.123)

"Prudent investors should consider purchasing only corporate bonds of the two highest grades, high-yield bonds have received so much attention that we need to discuss their attributes and why they are appropriate only for speculators, not investors." (p.125)

"The main purpose of fixed-income securities for most investors is to provide stability to their portfolio, allowing them to take equity risk. While it is true that high-yield debt has nonperfect correlation with equities, the correlation may increase at just the wrong time—when the distress risk of equities shows up." (p.128)

[6] This particular example was originally presented by Allan Roth in his article for CBSNEWS.com "Bonds vs. Bond Funds? An Easy Choice!", December 14, 2009.

[7] This chart is drawn from tabular data presented in the book Rational Investing In Irrational Times, by Larry E. Swedroe, 2002, p.141.

[8] Fidelity Learning Center, Four tips for bond investors. https://www.fidelity.com/viewpoints/four-tips-for-bond-investors

[9] Larry E. Swedroe, The Only Guide To A Winning Bond Strategy You'll Ever Need, 2006, p.30.

[10] This work in the 1950s was later given the name Modern Portfolio Theory. Harry M. Markowitz and later William F. Sharpe won Nobel Prizes for this important work which remain today the foundation of modern finance.

[11] Pillar nine from John C. Bogle's *The Twelve Pillars of Investment Wisdom*, www.vanguard.com/bogle_site/april272001.html

[12] http://www.depositaccounts.com/cd/5-year-cd-rates.html , Jan 2014

[13] http://research.stlouisfed.org/fred2/series/DGS5/

[14] See quotes from Larry Swedroe in note 5.

[15] "Bonds vs. Bond Funds? An Easy Choice!" by Allan Roth, www.cbsnews.com, December 14, 2009.

[16] Ibid.

[17] This comes from William J. Bernstein's explanation of "duration" http://www.efficientfrontier.com/ef/999/duration.htm

[18] The two portfolios are the Vanguard LifeStrategy Moderate Growth fund and the Vanguard Total Stock Market Index Adm fund, 1sep2007 through 9sep2012.

[19] [PDF] Handbook 20 - Basic Bond Analysis - Bank of England, Joanna Place, December 2000, p.35, www.bankofengland.co.uk/education/.../ccbshb20.pdf

[20] This comes from William J. Bernstein's explanation of "duration" http://www.efficientfrontier.com/ef/999/duration.htm

[21] Ibid.

[22] Ibid.

[23] http://www.investopedia.com/university/advancedbond/advancedbond5.asp

[24] To give it a name, so far we have been discussing the Macaulay definition of duration: *The present values of the bond's cash flows weighted by their time to receipt.* Yet another useful definition of *duration* is the ratio of price to yield change. That is, a bond with a 5-year duration will decrease 5% with each 1% increase in yield. For one reason, this second application uses a modified version of the Macaulay model that accounts for changing interest rates. If you divide the

Macaulay model by (1+Yield-to-Maturity) you will get the Modified duration. For most of us, and especially with low interest rates, these two versions of duration are approximately the same.

[25] www.bogleheads.org/wiki/Individual_Bonds_vs_a_Bond_Fund

[26] Specifically, the inflation number used in the Consumer Price Index for All Urban Consumers, Not Seasonally Adjusted (CPI-U NSA).

[27] Actually, this real interest rate is a composite of the real interest rate plus an inflation risk premium—but we have no way to ferret out what that inflation risk premium is. Conceptually, the TIPS yield is smaller than expected by this small premium that investors are willing to pay in order to guarantee their yield if inflation turns out to be bigger than expected.

[28] www.treasury.gov/resource-center/data-chart-center/interest-rates/Pages/Historic-Yield-Data-Visualization.aspx

[29] To be precise, bond expert Larry Swedroe points out the "the expected return of a TIPS should be slightly less than the expected return of a conventional U.S. Treasury security of the same maturity because investors in conventional Treasuries should receive a risk premium for bearing inflation risk. For example, the yield on a Treasury bond with ten years left to maturity might be 4 percent and the real yield on a TIPS with the same remaining term-to-maturity might be 2 percent. The difference between 4 and 2 percent reflects *both* the market's expectation of inflation for the period and a risk premium. While we currently have no way of separating the two, the inflation expectation might be 1.75 percent and the risk premium might be 0.25 percent."
Swedroe, Larry E., Guide To A Winning Bond Strategy, 2006, page 91-92.

[30] Bond expert Larry Swedroe discusses how this would work in his book. "Let's assume that the average maturity of three Vanguard funds is two, five, and eight years, respectively. Applying our rule of thumb, we would buy the fund with the highest yield, as long as it met the criteria of providing at least twenty basis points of extra yield for each year of extra maturity (due to the tax-exemption available on municipal bonds, the hurdle rate to extend would be perhaps just fifteen basis points)."
Swedroe, Larry E., Guide To A Winning Bond Strategy, 2006, p 77.

[31] Mapping: http://news.morningstar.com/articlenet/article.aspx?id=172614 , and some of the descriptive meanings from The Bond Book, Annette Thau, p33.

[32] Swedroe, Guide To A Winning Bonds Strategy, p 11

[33] The Fidelity Learning Center is an excellent resource with more about this and many other good tutorials: https://www.fidelity.com/learning-center/investment-products/fixed-income-bonds/what-is-a-bond

[34] www.bogleheads.org/wiki/Bond_Basics#Credit_quality

[35] https://www.fidelity.com/learning-center/investment-products/fixed-income-bonds/what-is-a-bond

[36] www.finra.org/Investors/InvestmentChoices/Bonds/SmartBondInvesting/Tips/

[37] Annette Thau, The Bond Book, Third Edition, 2011, p. 26

[38] Bogle, Common Sense on Mutual Funds, 1999, Page 14

[39] Ibid. page 60

[40] *Fixed Income's Low-Risk Anomaly*, Larry Swedroe
http://www.etf.com/sections/index-investor-corner/21862-swedroe-fixed-incomes-low-risk-anomaly.html

[41] Swedroe, Larry E., Guide to A Winning Bond Strategy, 2006, p 127

[42] Bogle, Common Sense on Mutual Funds, 1999, page 61

[43] Fidelity Learning Center, Four tips for bond investors.
https://www.fidelity.com/viewpoints/four-tips-for-bond-investors

[44] http://www.rickferri.com/blog/strategy/horseshoes-hand-grenades-and-asset-allocation/

[45] Benjamin Graham, in The Intelligent Investor. See also
http://www.bogleheads.org/wiki/Bogleheads%C2%AE_investment_philosophy

[46] John C. Bogle, The Clash of the Cultures: Investment vs. Speculation, 2012

[47] John C. Bogle, Keynote speech *"In Investing, You Get What You Don't Pay For"*, 2005, http://johncbogle.com/speeches/JCB_MS0205.pdf

[48]
http://www.finra.org/Investors/InvestmentChoices/Bonds/SmartBondInvesting/Tips/

[49] John C. Bogle, Common Sense on Mutual Funds, 1999, p 33.

[50] John C. Bogle, The Little Book of Common Sense Investing, 2007, p.37.

[51] The biggest of all the advantages that TIPS provide is to allow investors to earn the term premium (higher yields for longer maturities) without the risk of unexpected inflation.

[52] Mike Piper's blog "Oblivious Investor", Avoiding Big Investment Mistakes
http://www.obliviousinvestor.com/avoiding-big-investment-mistakes/

[53] "Investment Planning" article on Bogleheads website:

http://www.bogleheads.org/forum/viewtopic.php?f=1&t=6211

[54] "Asking Portfolio Questions" article on Bogleheads website:

http://www.bogleheads.org/forum/viewtopic.php?f=1&t=6212

[55] Norstad's paper can be found here:

www.norstad.org/finance/risk-and-time.html

[56] Ibid.

[57] Charles D. Ellis, Winning The Loser's Game, 5th Edition, McGraw Hill, 2010, p. 83.

[58] personal.vanguard.com/us/insights/investingtruths/investing-truth-about-risk

[59] "Bonds vs. Bond Funds? An Easy Choice!" by Allan Roth, www.cbsnews.com, December 14, 2009.

[60] A similar example is shown is this *Investing Essentials* primer by pkcrafter, a contribution that is well done and highly worth reading. http://investingroadmap.wordpress.com/

[61] Richard A. Ferri, CFA, "All About Index Funds", McGraw-Hill, 2007, p.25.

[62] Larry Swedroe, *Fixed Income's Low-Risk Anomaly*, April, 23, 2014 http://www.etf.com/sections/index-investor-corner/21862-swedroe-fixed-incomes-low-risk-anomaly.html

[63] Stefanie O'Connell, *Five Major Differences Between Cheap and Frugal*, http://money.usnews.com/money/the-frugal-shopper/2014/06/20/5-major-differences-between-cheap-and-frugal

[64] Vicki Robin and Joe Dominguez, *Your Money Or Your Life*, Penguin Books, 1992, pp. 54-56.

[65] Andrew Tobias, *The Only Investment Guide You'll Ever Need*, First Mariner Books edition 2010, p.13.

[66] Allan Roth, "Your financial net worth its about time not money", http://blog.aarp.org/2014/10/08/your-financial-net-worth-its-about-time-not-money/

Acknowledgements

It never ceases to amaze me how generous people are, both in sharing their time and their special talents.

I'd like to give a special thank-you to Larry Swedroe. Larry showed many of us how TIPS work and why they are interesting. I am honored that he contributed some opening pages to this booklet.

William Bernstein is the author that caused me to look up from my career and think about my retirement investments. His endorsement is special to me.

If I had written this book a few years earlier it wouldn't have included the discussion about CDs, but Allan Roth showed me how they can be attractive. I am indebted to him for this and because he has a gift for simple explanations.

Taylor Larimore is the epitome of the multitude of selfless people who spend hours each day helping new investors hear wisdom amid the noise. Taylor is a founder of this group that call themselves Bogleheads. His supportive words played a big part in encouraging me to grab the baton and start spreading this time-proven wisdom by making free online videos.

I have two new friends, Barb Dewey and Paul Keck, who get a huge thank you from me for proofreading my manuscript.

Also, I give a warm shout-out to long-time friends Linda Mahagan, Jon Noble, and Rob and Wendy Stafford for their help and feedback.

But I reserve my biggest thank you to Jennifer Howell who reads and watches my first drafts (books and videos) and sends me back to the drawing board when I get lazy and let lingo and jargon creep into my explanations. She's the best.

About the Author

Rick Van Ness is a successful private investor and retired executive who provides investor education through online videos, short books, and workshops. Rick has an engineering degree from Cornell University and a MBA in Finance from New York University. His background in engineering and business provides him with the excellent basis for understanding and teaching about investments and financial planning.

Rick provides unbiased education. He helps students understand the teachings of the most widely respected economists and financial planners. Students learn that investing smart is simple (not easy) and to take charge of their own finances on their paths to achieving rich and fulfilling lives. He is President of GrowthConnection LLC.

Neither Rick Van Ness nor GrowthConnection LLC sell any investment products or services, and do not provide individual investment advice. He educates you without self-interest (other than the joy he always gets from hearing from readers).

Connect with me online!

Website: **www.FinancingLife.org**
Email: rick@financinglife.org

149

Index

If you enjoyed this book, you might also like:

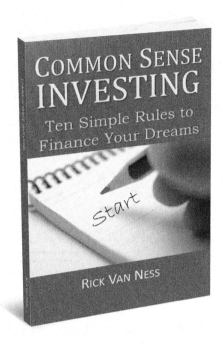

The ten rules are:

1. Develop a workable plan
2. Invest early and often
3. Never bear too much or too little risk
4. Diversify!
5. Never try to time the market
6. Use index funds when possible
7. Keep costs low
8. Minimize taxes
9. Keep it simple
10. Stay the course

Change a Life!

If you've said to yourself "I wish I had read this book when I was younger," take a minute right now to buy a copy of this book for someone you know who is that age now. You can make a huge difference in a young person's life today.

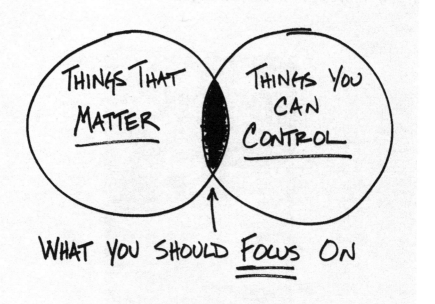

Sketch by Carl Richards at BehaviorGap.com

This sketch reminds me that life is short, and filled with everyday miracles. Money plays an important role, but it doesn't need to be complicated. Use common sense investing, and then get out and enjoy life! Thank you Carl Richards for all your precious sketches.

The favor of a review...

Has this book been helpful?

Reviews, ratings and comments about this guide on Amazon, or on your favorite blog, are much appreciated. If you've enjoyed the walk, you can leave a review here:

www.amazon.com/dp/0985800402

Here are three reasons you might consider for leaving a review:
- Reviews help others to find this book, and decide whether to read it.
- You help me to sell more books. *This is how we pay for the direct expenses of this not-for-profit educational project (for which I volunteer my time).*
- I get to hear what you think. *I read all the reviews of my books and love to hear what readers have to say.*

If you enjoyed this book, I would REALLY appreciate you putting up a one or two sentence review on Amazon.

Simply click where it says "xx customer reviews" next to the overall star rating, then click the button "Write a customer review."

Thank you so much!

If you're reading on a Kindle device, you'll also have a chance to rate the book and share your rating with your friends on Facebook and Twitter when you turn the last page...

Made in the USA
Middletown, DE
10 January 2021

31245348R00096